A PICKLE AND CHUTNEY COOKBOOK

DIGBY LAW (1936–1987) was a pioneer with New Zealand food, taking what grew in our gardens and suggesting new ways of eating it and, at the same time, lining it up with the best food available from overseas. His positive encouragement has led many mediocre cooks to a true appreciation of ingredients and cooking methods, flavours and presentation.

Digby was well known as a writer and broadcaster on food, with a regular column in *Auckland Metro* magazine. He prepared food for photography and television commercials and was a cookery consultant and demonstrator. He has written six culinary publications, including the much-acclaimed and best-selling A VEGETABLE COOKBOOK, A SOUP COOKBOOK, DIGBY LAW'S ENTREE COOKBOOK and A DESSERT COOKBOOK.

A PICKLE AND CHUTNEY COOKBOOK

Digby Law

Hodder & Stoughton
AUCKLAND LONDON SYDNEY TORONTO

Typeset by Glenfield Graphics Ltd, Auckland.
Printed and bound by Singapore National Printers Ltd for
Hodder and Stoughton Ltd, 46 View Road, Glenfield,
Auckland, New Zealand.

Contents

Measurements used in this book are metric. The cup is a standard 250 ml, the tablespoon is 15 ml, and the teaspoon is 5 ml. All cup and spoon measures are level.

Thanks to the many, many people whose generous help and advice was absolutely invaluable and to others whose generous help and advice was a highly delightful hindrance.

Introduction

Pickles, chutneys and other savoury preserves have been around for centuries. Chutneys are derived from the Indian *chatni* and pickles and ketchups were originally from the Orient. Down through the history of civilisation they have all been adapted and modified to suit western palates and styles of eating. That old, attractive term 'relishes' is still the best way to describe these delicacies, which by their combinations of flavours give relish or 'zing' to basic foods.

Everyone is familiar with the piquant effect of traditional partnerships like cold meat and chutney, cheese and pickles, or sausages and tomato sauce—but this volume offers many different relishes and a wide use for them all, to enhance the creative side of your cooking.

All nations seem to have their own preferred relishes. It is interesting to note that 'pickles' to an American invariably means dill pickles, or a version of pickled cucumbers. To the English a pickle is a dark brown, fruit chutney, like the one that goes so well with the ploughman's lunch. To a New Zealander or an Australian a pickle is usually yellow and flavoured with mustard.

Pickles and chutneys are easy to make. Unlike jams, where even experienced cooks can make ghastly mistakes, pickles and chutneys are very rewarding and quite simple to make. The methods are straightforward, the materials usually cheap and plentiful, and the results reliably excellent. Nothing is more useful in the pantry than a shelf of home-made condiments, not only to make ordinary foods quite exotic (try pickled fruits with leftover ham, or a chutney with cold lamb) but also in the preparation of sauces. It is good to be able to offer a plate of crisp pickles for guests to nibble, along with biscuits and cheese and pre-dinner drinks.

Pickles and chutneys are simple to prepare because in savoury preserves, as in other savoury dishes, the quantities are not really too critical. If you have a little fruit or some vegetable leftovers, it is possible to just add them to the recipe.

7

If you happen to double up on the spices by mistake: hold your breath, it could well turn out the creation of the century. The recipes are here as guidelines, indicating the ratio of solids to liquids, sweeteners to spices, or preservatives to the preserved.

Try the recipes first, and later you may decide that you could improve upon them in your own way. They have all been tested. If you take into account moisture content, time of cooking, rate of cooking, freshness of ingredients and so on, these recipes will work for you. If you find a particular combination of spices, vinegar and sugar which is very much to your taste, then try it out as a basis for other pickles and chutneys, too.

Where possible the names of these 'relishes' have been kept simple and straightforward, while some classic names for some pickles and chutneys have of course remained unchanged. Do not be confused if you have seen some recipes given under other names elsewhere. Chefs and cookery writers all love playing with names and transposing them, and so do people who believe that if you give something an unusual name it will disguise the fact that it is very ordinary, if not deadly dull! The names used here have been kept as close to the original ingredients as possible.

'Relishes' are fascinating: as with many other dishes, often the simplest combinations taste the most complex. On the other hand, remember that complex combinations, on long keeping, usually taste superb in the end.

Most chutneys and pickles are best kept for a month or so to allow the flavours to mellow and mature. Sauces should be kept for a few weeks at least, while relishes can be eaten immediately. Mustards are best left for a week or so, while vinegars are ready as soon as they are made. There are many exceptions to these rules, and all are stated in the recipes concerned. Some chutneys and sauces, provided they are properly sealed, will keep for many years. All savoury preserves should be carefully checked after six months.

The storage of chutneys and pickles is quite important. A cool, dark place is best. The coolest cupboard in a room is at the bottom near the floor, not up towards the ceiling. Hot air rises and those top cupboards can get very warm indeed. The jars are best kept at a moderately cool, even temperature: not only does this keep the ingredients in a stable condition, but if the jars are not completely sealed then evaporation is much slower in the cool.

When chutneys and pickles or sauces and so on go *off* they smell it and often look it too. If they smell good and taste good then you can be almost certain that they are still in good condition. If in doubt, throw them out.

The yield in making these recipes can vary considerably. The ripeness of the fruit, the size of the saucepan, the speed or slowness of the cooking, all contribute to the end result. So it is a good idea to have a few extra jars or bottles sterilised and ready in case the yield is greater than indicated.

Most recipes used here can be successfully halved. The resulting amounts of each recipe all tend to be different and are mainly determined by the amount of base ingredients used.

Some recipes suggest salting the ingredients before cooking. Not only does this draw out some of the moisture, but salt also acts as an antiseptic, destroying bacteria. Vinegar is the main preservative, and sugar and spices are also, to a mild degree. If you are sprinkling vegetables or fruit with salt and allowing them to stand for a time, and if you are unsure of the amount of salt to add, use your discretion, as foods can always be rinsed to remove the salt. Extra salt can be added later, towards the end of cooking time, if you think it necessary.

Never put hot liquid in cold glass. To heat the jars, it is easiest to stand them in some hot water in the sink, a few minutes before filling. Any spillage goes into the sink and eliminates mess and you can wash the outside of the jars there and then. Put the lids in the hot water, too, to act as a mild steriliser. Make sure you label the jars as soon as possible. Write on the date of making, and the maturity date, if necessary. The latest finds, like kiwanos, carambolas, and so on are all too expensive at the moment to make into pickles. A pity, as they would be good for this purpose, since they are not really much fun by themselves.

A Few Assumptions
Unless otherwise stated use white *sugar*. White sugar is good for clear pickles and light-coloured chutneys and sauces, whereas brown sugar gives a good dark colour and tends to add a slight caramel taste.

If the *vinegar* type is not stipulated, the choice is yours. Malt vinegar is good for everyday chutneys and sauces. White, wine or cider vinegars are better for more delicate chutneys and sauces and most pickles.

Dry *mustard* or simply mustard means powdered mustard. *Mustard seed* means yellow mustard unless otherwise stated.

It is presumed that all raisins now available are seedless.

Green and red peppers are sweet peppers or capsicums. *Chillies* are chilli peppers. Onions should be peeled.

All fruit and vegetables should be ripe unless otherwise stated. They should also be in sound condition.

Pickling spice — a mixture of whole spices — is bought as such. You can, however, put together a mixture of your favourite whole spices if you wish.

Mixed spice is ground mixed spice which is bought as such.

A Word on Equipment

Make pickles and chutneys in an aluminium, stainless steel or enamel-lined pan. A preserving pan or large saucepan is ideal. Brass and copper react with vinegar and should not be used. Glass jars are worth saving. Screw-top jars are ideal, especially those with plastic lids or plastic-lined metal lids. Metal lids, unless plastic-lined, will react with the vinegar in the pickle and corrode the lid and discolour the pickle. For complete sealing use melted paraffin wax on top of the pickle before putting on the lid. Agee seals are an easier method for sealing jars completely. Fill the jar as full as possible with the hot contents, place the Agee dome seal on the jar and screw on the metal band to hold the seal down until it seals. Remove the band when the jar is cool. This is known as sealing by the overflow method.

Sieves, funnels, slotted spoons and weighing scales are all useful equipment. And a food processor, a mincer, a blender or liquidiser and a vegetable mill can all help to save time in their own ways.

To sterilise jars, wash and thoroughly rinse them. They can then be stood on a rack in a large pan of boiling water and simmered for 15 minutes. Remove the jars and put in a warm oven to dry. Alternatively, the washed and rinsed jars can be placed in an oven at 120°C for about 30 minutes.

The Chutneys

The word chutney is Indian in origin, and derives from the word *chatni*. In India *chatni* are spiced relishes served alongside the bland *dhal* or lentil dishes. Indians like their *chatni* both cooked and uncooked, and we have adapted them so that we have long-keeping chutneys, fresh chutneys and refrigerator chutneys.

Although the best chutneys are probably made from fruit, there are some very good vegetable-based ones. A chutney is a thick pulp, and not a mixture in which the fruit or vegetable is instantly recognisable: for this reason, chow chow, piccalilli, and so on are to be found in the pickle section of this book. And just to confuse you, some chutneys have been called pickles, often because the name sounds better, though the consistency of the 'pickle' will be a heavy purée like that of a chutney. The line between chutneys and pickles is so fine, anyway, that having chosen a particular ingredient you should consult both the pickle and chutney sections in the index to choose the most suitable recipe.

Is chutney a savoury jam, or is a jam a sweet chutney? The former definition is correct, but many chutneys can be both sweet and savoury, and are sometimes eaten the way jam is traditionally eaten.

When not stated, chutneys are cooked uncovered. Remember that it is better to have a chutney too thin than too thick when it is cooked, because some ingredients continue absorbing liquid for some time after cooking, and unless the jar is absolutely airtight, there will always be some evaporation. To tell if a chutney is ready to bottle, you can test it like jam: spoon a little onto a cold saucer and if it becomes soft jelly, then it is ready. Another indication is when the chutney starts to catch on the bottom of the saucepan. And yet another is when a thin film of liquid separates out above the chutney in the saucepan.

Some chutneys should keep for a long, long time, while others last no more than six months. If the chutney is heavy in vinegar, sugar and spices, it should keep well, and this sort of chutney is invariably better the longer it is kept. Mild chutneys have a much shorter life span but reach their best often a few days or a few weeks after being made.

Chutneys have many uses. With cold meats and cheeses, whether by themselves, or in sandwiches, they are indispensable. But there are other ways with chutneys too: they can give 'zing' to stews and casseroles; and chutneys make excellent curry accompaniments or with fish or chicken, hot meat or vegetables. Brush chutney on chicken pieces, chops or steak when grilling or barbecuing, 5 minutes before the end of cooking time. Chutneys can be used in canapés too, or as a dipping sauce for meat balls or cheese balls.

Apple Chutney

Serve this mildly spiced chutney with chicken or seafood curry dishes, or with roast pork or cold pork or ham.

1 kg apples
500g onions
500g sultanas
1 cup brown sugar
3 cups white vinegar
½ teaspoon dry mustard
½ teaspoon ground ginger
½ teaspoon salt
pinch cayenne pepper

Peel and core the apples, peel the onions and chop them finely. Combine all the ingredients in a large saucepan. Bring to the boil and cook gently, covered, for about 1 hour until the mixture is tender and thickened. Add a little more vinegar if necessary.

Pour into hot, clean jars and seal.
Makes about 2 litres.

Apple and Date Chutney

This is a sweet, thick chutney that makes an excellent sandwich filling and goes especially well with cheese.

1 kg cooking apples
500g onions
500g dates
250g brown sugar
1 teaspoon salt
1 teaspoon dry mustard
½ teaspoon ground ginger
½ teaspoon ground allspice
2½ cups malt vinegar

Peel, core and slice the apples. Finely chop the onions and dates. Combine all the ingredients in a large saucepan, bring to the boil and cook gently, covered, for 45 minutes to 1 hour. Stir the chutney often as it is quite thick and may burn. Add a little more vinegar if necessary.

Pour into hot, clean jars and seal.
Makes about 3 litres.

Apple and Plum Chutney

Good with any meats and ideal in sandwiches or in scones.

2 kg apples, peeled and cored
1 kg plums, stoned
500g onions
250g sultanas
300g brown sugar
6 tablespoons dry mustard
4 tablespoons ground ginger
1 teaspoon cayenne pepper
2 tablespoons salt
2 litres malt vinegar

Finely chop the apples, plums and onions. Combine with the

rest of the ingredients in a large saucepan. Bring to the boil and cook very slowly for about 3 hours or until the chutney is thick.

Pour into hot, clean jars and seal.

Makes about 4 litres.

Apple and Red Pepper Chutney

Sweetish and mild, and especially pleasant with cheese.

1.5 kg apples
3 red or green peppers
1 medium onion
1 cup raisins
3 lemons
1 tablespoon salt
2 cups white vinegar
1½ cups sugar
1½ teaspoons ground ginger

Peel and core the apples, de-seed the peppers, peel the onion and mince them all together with the raisins.

Place them all in a saucepan. Add the juice and grated rind of the lemons, then add the salt, vinegar, sugar and ginger. Bring to the boil and cook gently for about 1 hour or until the chutney is thick.

Pour into hot, clean jars and seal when cold.

Makes about 3 litres.

Apple and Tomato Chutney

This is quite hot, so, for a medium chutney, halve the amount of cayenne pepper.

1 kg apples, peeled, cored and finely chopped
1 kg tomatoes, peeled and coarsely chopped
500g onions, finely chopped
4 cloves garlic, finely chopped
1 cup raisins
1 tablespoon salt
1 teaspoon cayenne pepper
1 tablespoon ground ginger
1½ cups brown sugar
3 cups malt vinegar

Prepare the apples, tomatoes, onions and garlic, and combine them in a large saucepan with the rest of the ingredients. Boil gently for about 2 hours, stirring often, until the chutney is quite thick.

Pour into hot, clean jars and seal when cold.
Makes about 3.5 litres.

Apple and Walnut Chutney

A sort of savoury Christmas mincemeat that is ideal with all cold meats.

2 kg apples
500g raisins
6 whole cloves
1 cup chopped walnuts
2½ cups cider vinegar
2 oranges
2 lemons
1 kg brown sugar

Peel, core and chop the apples finely. Chop the raisins and cook with the apples, cloves, walnuts and vinegar until the apples and raisins are soft.

Grate the rind of the oranges and lemons and add to the cooked ingredients together with the orange and lemon juice and the sugar. Simmer until thick, then spoon into hot, clean jars and seal.

Makes about 2.5 litres.

Minted Apple Chutney

Absolutely marvellous with lamb, curries and cold meats. Good, too, with cold meat in sandwiches.

50g mint leaves
500g apples, peeled and cored
250g tomatoes, peeled
250g onions, peeled
350g raisins
1¾ cups cider vinegar
2 cups sugar
2 teaspoons salt
1 teaspoon dry mustard

Finely chop, or mince, the mint leaves, apples, tomatoes, onions and raisins.

In a large saucepan heat the vinegar, sugar, salt and mustard. Bring to the boil and add the finely chopped ingredients. Mix well and boil, uncovered, for 20 minutes.

Pour into hot, clean jars and seal.

Apricot Chutney

Terrific with cheese or in sandwiches.

3 kg apricots
1 kg onions
750g sugar
2 teaspoons salt
1 teaspoon whole cloves
1 teaspoon black peppercorns
1 teaspoon ground mace
1 teaspoon curry powder
½ teaspoon cayenne pepper
4 cups malt vinegar

Remove the stones and coarsely chop the apricots. Finely chop the onions. Combine all the ingredients in a large saucepan and boil slowly for 1 hour, stirring often, especially towards the end of cooking time.
 Pour into hot, clean jars and seal.
Makes about 3.5 litres.

Apricot, Carrot and Swede Chutney

An unusual flavour with a real bite makes this a fascinating chutney.

400g dried apricots
5 cups malt vinegar
500g carrots
500g swede turnips
500g onions
250g brown sugar
2 teaspoons ground mace
2 teaspoons cayenne pepper

Soak the apricots overnight in 2 cups vinegar.
 Next day, drain, reserving the vinegar and chop the apricots finely. Peel the carrots, turnips and onions and finely chop

them. Combine all the ingredients in a large saucepan, including the reserved vinegar. Bring to the boil and cook slowly, uncovered, stirring occasionally, for about 1 hour. Add more vinegar if it gets too thick.

Spoon into hot, clean jars and seal.

Makes about 3.5 litres.

Apricot and Chilli Chutney

Bland apricots and hot chillies make yet another exciting contrast.

250g dried apricots
6 chillies, chopped
250g brown sugar
1 teaspoon salt
1 small piece fresh ginger, sliced finely
600 ml white vinegar

Soak the apricots overnight in water to cover.

Next day, cook in the same water until the apricots are soft. Add the remaining ingredients and simmer gently, uncovered, for 30 minutes.

Pour into hot, clean jars and seal.

Makes about 1 litre.

Apricot and Date Chutney

An excellent chutney using dried fruits so it can be made at any time of the year.

500g dried apricots
1 kg stoned dates
500g sultanas
250g preserved ginger, finely chopped
4 cloves garlic, crushed
500g brown sugar
3 tablespoons salt
½ teaspoon cayenne pepper
white vinegar

Soak the apricots overnight in water to cover.

Drain, place all the ingredients in a large saucepan, cover with vinegar, and mix well. Bring to the boil and cook very slowly for 2 hours, until a good brown colour and thick. If too thick, add more vinegar during cooking.

Spoon into hot, clean jars and seal.

Makes about 5 litres.

Apricot and Raisin Chutney

A sweet chutney that is a perfect foil for hot curries and tasty cheeses.

250g dried apricots
2 cups boiling water
200g raisins
1½ cups brown sugar
1 cup white vinegar
6 whole cloves
2 teaspoons mustard seeds

Cover the apricots with the boiling water and let stand for at least 2 hours.

Put the apricots and liquid in a saucepan with the remaining ingredients. Stir over low heat until the sugar is dissolved, then bring to the boil. Reduce heat and simmer, uncovered, for 1 hour or until mixture is thick.

Pour into hot, clean jars and seal.

Makes about 1 litre.

Babaco Chutney

Sweet, spicy and aromatic—superb with cold meats and cheeses, and bliss with curries. Semi-ripe, de-seeded tropical pawpaw can be substituted for the babaco.

1.5 kg half-ripe babaco
1 kg tomatoes
2 chillies
500g sultanas
25g root ginger
25g garlic
1 onion
2 tablespoons salt
3 cups white vinegar
1 cup lemon or lime juice
2 tablespoons mustard seed
1 kg sugar

Peel the babaco and tomatoes. In a mincer or food processor mince the babaco, tomatoes, chillies, sultanas, root ginger, garlic and onion. Put the ingredients in a large saucepan and add the salt, vinegar, lemon juice and mustard seed. Mix well, bring to the boil and cook for about 30 minutes. Add the sugar, and cook, stirring often, until the required jam consistency.

Pour into hot, clean jars and seal.

Makes about 4 litres.

Banana Chutney

An ideal accompaniment to curry or a delicious spread on toast.

4 medium onions
6 bananas
1 cup chopped dates
1½ cups vinegar
½ cup chopped crystallised ginger
1 teaspoon salt
1 teaspoon curry powder
1 cup raisins
⅓ cup sugar
2 cups water

Finely chop the onions and mash the bananas. Place in a large saucepan with the dates and vinegar. Simmer, stirring occasionally, for 20 minutes.

Add the ginger, salt, curry powder, raisins, sugar and water. Cook very gently, stirring often, for about 40 minutes, until thick.

Spoon into hot, clean jars and seal.
Makes about 1.5 litres.

Beetroot and Mint Chutney

Use with sliced cold meat, in chicken or ham sandwiches, or with bread and cheese.

1.25 kg beetroot, cooked, peeled and finely chopped
250g raisins, finely chopped
2 onions, finely chopped
1 tablespoon salt
1 tablespoon ground allspice
4 whole black peppercorns
150g brown sugar
2 cups white vinegar
2 tablespoons finely chopped fresh mint

Prepare the beetroot. Combine the raisins, onions, salt, allspice, peppercorns, sugar, vinegar and mint in a saucepan and bring to the boil. Lower heat, cover and simmer for about 1 hour until the mixture has thickened. Stir the mixture often to prevent sticking.

Add the prepared beetroot and simmer for a further 20 minutes until all the ingredients are thoroughly blended. Remove from heat and allow to cool.

Spoon into clean jars and seal.

Makes about 2 litres.

Bengal Chutney

This one is hot and spicy and good with all the foods that chutneys complement. The longer the chutney is kept — within reason — the better it becomes.

1.5–2 kg sour apples
500g onions
50g garlic
100g fresh ginger
250g raisins
100g mustard seed
1 teaspoon cayenne pepper
2 tablespoons salt
500g brown sugar
7 cups malt vinegar

Peel and core the apples and peel the onions and garlic. Mince together the apples, onions, garlic, ginger, raisins and mustard seed in a mincer or food processor.

Combine all the ingredients in a large saucepan, bring to the boil and cook gently, uncovered, for about 1 hour, until pulped and thick.

Spoon into hot, clean jars and seal.

Makes about 4 litres.

Blackberry Chutney

An excellent chutney for cold meats or with hot pork, duck or goose. Blueberries, boysenberries, raspberries or loganberries could be substituted for the blackberries.

500g cooking apples
250g onions
1.5 kg blackberries
2 teaspoons ground ginger
½ teaspoon dry mustard
½ teaspoon ground mace
1 teaspoon salt
500g brown sugar
2 cups white vinegar

Peel, core and finely chop the apples, peel and finely chop the onions. In a large saucepan combine the apples, onions and blackberries with the remaining ingredients.

Slowly bring to the boil, stirring, until the sugar is dissolved. Simmer for about 1 hour until the desired consistency. This type of chutney is better more liquid than too dry.

Pour into hot, clean jars and seal.
Makes about 3 litres.

Blackcurrant Chutney

A rich, sweet yet pleasantly spiced chutney, that is not only good with lamb or beef, but also with cheese *and* as an ice-cream topping.

500g blackcurrants
500g brown sugar
125g raisins, chopped
2 tablespoons mustard
1 tablespoon ground ginger
1 tablespoon salt

1 small onion, grated
1 cup malt vinegar

Combine all the ingredients in a large saucepan. Bring to the boil and cook gently for about 30 minutes, until thick.
Pour into hot, clean jars and seal when cold.
Makes about 1.5 litres.

Blueberry Chutney

Sweet and spicy, and marvellous with cold poultry, pork or game. Or try it in cheese sandwiches or with vanilla ice-cream. Cranberries or redcurrants could be substituted for the blueberries.

500g fresh or frozen blueberries
1 tart apple, peeled, cored and diced
2 cups brown sugar
¾ cup white vinegar
½ cup chopped mixed peel
½ teaspoon salt
¼ teaspoon ground ginger
¼ teaspoon ground cloves
¼ teaspoon ground allspice
¼ teaspoon dry mustard

Combine all the ingredients in a large saucepan. Slowly bring to the boil, stirring, until the sugar is dissolved. Boil gently for about 20 minutes, or until the mixture has reached a jam consistency.
Spoon into hot, clean jars and seal.
Makes about 1 litre.

Carrot and Apple Chutney

Sweetish and gingery, and excellent with cheese.

250g carrots
250g apples
50g raisins
1 small onion, peeled
125g brown sugar
1 teaspoon salt
1 teaspoon ground ginger
¾ cup malt vinegar

Grate the carrots, peel and dice the apples, and finely chop the raisins and onion. Mix all the ingredients together in a saucepan. Bring to the boil and cook gently, stirring often, until thick and pulped.

Spoon into hot, clean jars and seal.
Makes about 750 ml.

Indian Carrot Chutney

This can be used immediately and is excellent with curries or with cheeses.

1 kg carrots
1 tablespoon salt
4 cloves garlic, thinly sliced
2 tablespoons mustard seeds
2 teaspoons cumin seeds
small piece fresh root ginger, finely chopped
1 tablespoon black peppercorns
1 cup brown sugar
1¼ cups white vinegar

Wash, scrape and trim the carrots and finely chop them. Place the carrots with the remaining ingredients in a large saucepan and bring to the boil. Simmer gently, covered, until the carrots are tender.

Allow the mixture to cool before bottling and sealing.
Makes about 2 litres.

Cherry Chutney

This is a delicious dark red chutney. Leave out the nuts if you wish but they do make the chutney something special.

700g fresh cherries
2½ cups white wine vinegar
350g apples, peeled, cored and chopped
1 large onion, finely chopped
1 teaspoon ground ginger
2 teaspoons salt
2 tablespoons pickling spice
1 cup brown sugar
2 tablespoons clear honey
1 cup chopped nuts

Wash the cherries, remove the stalks, and simmer in 1¼ cups white wine vinegar until soft. Allow to cool enough to handle, then remove and discard the stones.

Return the cherries to the same saucepan and vinegar, and add the apples, onion, ginger and salt. Tie the pickling spice in muslin. Add and cook until the fruit is tender, then add the remaining vinegar, the sugar and honey. Stir to dissolve the sugar, then cook very gently, stirring occasionally, until thick. Add the nuts and remove the spice bag.

Pour into hot, clean jars and seal.
Makes about 2 litres.

Chilli Chutney

This is red hot, so put it in small jars and remember a little goes a long way.

250g fresh red chillies
8 cloves garlic
5cm piece fresh ginger
2 cups malt vinegar
2 cups white sugar
3 teaspoons salt

Remove the cores and most of the seeds from the chillies. Use rubber gloves unless you don't mind the chilli juice getting under the fingernails and stinging.

Peel the garlic and mince the chillies, garlic and ginger. Combine with the remaining ingredients in a saucepan and boil very gently, uncovered, for about 1 hour, or until the chutney is getting quite thick.

Pour into small, hot, clean jars and seal.

Choko Chutney

A sweetish, mild chutney.

4 chokos
2 cooking apples
2 tomatoes
3 medium onions
2 cups sugar
1 tablespoon salt
pinch cayenne pepper
½ teaspoon ground cloves
1½ cups mixed dried fruit
2½ cups malt vinegar

Peel and core the chokos and apples, peel the tomatoes and onions, and finely chop them all. Combine with the remaining ingredients in a large saucepan, bring to the boil and cook very gently, stirring occasionally, for about 1½-2 hours, until the chutney is thickened.

Pour into hot, clean jars and seal.

Makes about 2.5 litres.

Courgette and Apple Chutney

A sweet chutney ideal with tasty cheese, in sandwiches, on toast or with cold meats.

1.5 kg courgettes
2 teaspoons salt
1.5 kg apples
500g onions
750g sugar
2 litres vinegar
2 teaspoons dry mustard
2 teaspoons ginger
¾ teaspoon ground black pepper
juice of 1 lemon

Slice the courgettes finely, place them in a bowl, sprinkle with the salt and let stand overnight.

Peel and finely chop the apples and onions. Combine with the courgettes in a large saucepan. Add the remaining ingredients, bring to the boil and cook very slowly for about 2 hours, until the mixture is thick.

Spoon into hot, clean jars and seal.

Makes about 4 litres.

Cucumber Chutney

A lightly spiced chutney with the refreshing flavour of cucumber.

3 kg cucumbers, peeled and sliced
1.5 kg onions, halved and sliced
1 tablespoon salt
250g sultanas
1.5 kg brown sugar
2 teaspoons ground ginger
½ teaspoon cayenne pepper
6 cups malt vinegar
1 teaspoon peppercorns
1 teaspoon whole allspice
½ teaspoon whole cloves

Combine the cucumber and onion in a bowl. Sprinkle with the salt and let stand overnight.

Next day, drain the vegetables well. In a saucepan combine the vegetables with the sultanas, brown sugar, ginger, cayenne pepper and vinegar.

Tie the peppercorns, allspice and cloves in muslin and add to the saucepan. Bring to the boil and cook very slowly for about 1 hour or until thickened. Discard the spice bag.

Pour into hot, clean jars and seal.
Makes about 6 litres.

Date Chutney

This chutney can be used as soon as it is made. Especially good with cheese.

1 kg pitted dates
2 small chillies
500g onions
250g sultanas
4 cloves garlic

1 teaspoon salt
1 teaspoon ground ginger
½ teaspoon cracked black pepper
2 litres white vinegar

Finely chop the dates, chillies and onions. Put them in a large saucepan with the sultanas.

Finely chop the garlic and crush it to a paste with the salt. Add to the saucepan together with the remaining ingredients. Mix well, then bring to the boil and cook very slowly for 1–1½ hours, until the chutney is thick.

Spoon into hot, clean jars and seal.

Makes about 3.5 litres.

Feijoa Chutney

Aromatic fruits such as feijoas make excellent chutneys.

1 kg feijoas
500g onions
300g raisins
500g pitted dates
500g brown sugar
1 tablespoon ground ginger
1 tablespoon curry powder
1 teaspoon ground cloves
¼ teaspoon cayenne pepper
4 teaspoons salt
4 cups malt vinegar

Wipe the feijoas, trim the ends and finely slice them by hand. Finely chop the onions and coarsely chop the raisins and dates. Combine all the ingredients in a large saucepan, bring to the boil and cook very gently for 1½–2 hours, until the chutney is thick. Make sure the chutney doesn't catch on the bottom of the saucepan.

Pour into hot, clean jars and seal.

Makes about 3 litres.

Fresh Fig Chutney

A sweet spicy chutney with the wonderful earthy flavour of the figs featuring prominently. Superb with cheeses.

750g ripe fresh figs
75g pitted dates
50g crystallised ginger
250g onions
2½ cups malt vinegar
150g brown sugar
75g raisins
½ teaspoon salt
¼ teaspoon cayenne pepper

Slice the figs and finely chop the dates, ginger and onions. Bring the vinegar and sugar to the boil.

Combine all the other ingredients together in another saucepan. Pour the hot vinegar mixture over, mix well and let stand overnight.

Next day, bring the chutney to the boil, and cook very slowly for about 3 hours, until it is thick and dark.

Spoon into hot, clean jars and seal.

Makes about 1.5 litres.

Gooseberry Chutney

Another all-purpose chutney, using the tart flavour of gooseberries in a sweet-sour-spicy pickling mixture. This is also known as *Cashmere Chutney.*

1 kg gooseberries
25g garlic or 2 large onions, finely chopped
5 cups malt vinegar
500g raisins
500g dates, finely chopped
125g crystallised ginger, finely chopped
1 kg brown sugar

2 tablespoons salt
½ teaspoon cayenne pepper
½ teaspoon ground cinnamon

Top and tail the gooseberries. Combine them in a large saucepan with the garlic and vinegar, bring to the boil, and boil for 10 minutes. Add the remaining ingredients and boil for a further 10 minutes, stirring occasionally. Let stand for about 30 minutes, stirring occasionally, until the chutney is fairly thick.

Pour into warm, clean jars and seal.
Makes about 4 litres.

Gooseberry and Prune Chutney

Tangy gooseberries combine well with sweetish prunes.

1 kg gooseberries
500g pitted prunes, chopped
500g onions, halved and sliced
500g raisins
1 tablespoon ground ginger
¼ teaspoon cayenne pepper
1 teaspoon salt
5 cups malt vinegar
500g brown sugar

Top and tail the gooseberries and put in a large saucepan with the other ingredients except the sugar. Boil for about 1 hour, stirring often, until the fruit is pulpy. Add the brown sugar, stir until dissolved and boil for a further minute.

Pour into hot, clean jars and seal.
Makes about 4 litres.

Cape Gooseberry Chutney

Green gooseberries can also be used for this interesting chutney.

6 cups cape gooseberries, chopped
2 teaspoons salt
½ teaspoon cayenne pepper
250g raisins, chopped
500g onions, minced
1 tablespoon ground ginger
1 tablespoon dry mustard
500g sugar
5 cups malt vinegar

Combine all the ingredients in a large saucepan. Heat the mixture slowly, then simmer for 1½-2 hours, until thick.
   Pour into small, hot, clean jars and seal.
   Makes about 2.5 litres.

Grape Chutney

The type of grape used will make a difference to the flavour of the chutney. Sweet, white grapes make a tangy, fruity chutney, especially good with cheese.

3 kg ripe grapes
1 kg sharp apples, peeled and chopped
1 kg onions, finely chopped
500g raisins
1 kg sugar
50g whole pickling spice (in muslin bag)
100g salt
2 teaspoons white pepper
2.5 litres white vinegar

Place all the ingredients in a large saucepan or preserving pan. Bring to the boil and boil slowly, uncovered, for 3 hours. Skim off the pips as they rise.
   Discard the pickling spice and pour the chutney into hot,

clean jars and seal.
Makes about 6 litres.

Grapefruit Chutney

The sweeter the grapefruit the better for this intriguing bitter-sweet chutney. It will be quite liquid but should thicken on standing.

1 kg grapefruit pulp
2 teaspoons ground cloves
1 cup malt vinegar
750g sugar
250g raisins
50g brazil nuts, finely chopped

Prepare the pulp from fresh grapefruit.

In a saucepan combine the grapefruit pulp, ground cloves, vinegar, sugar and raisins. Bring to the boil, stirring to dissolve the sugar, then simmer gently, uncovered, for about 1 hour, until fairly thick. Add the finely chopped brazil nuts. Heat to boiling, then allow to cool, stirring occasionally.

Spoon into clean jars and seal.
Makes about 1.5 litres.

Green Pepper Chutney

Sweet and mildly spiced, this goes well with traditional meats such as roast lamb or pork. Try it with cold meats or hamburgers too. In the United States, green pepper chutney is known as chilli chutney.

1.25 kg green peppers, cored, seeded and finely chopped
500g onions, finely chopped
2 tablespoons olive oil
1 kg very ripe tomatoes, peeled and chopped
1 clove garlic, crushed
250g sultanas
1 teaspoon ground ginger
1 teaspoon ground mixed spice
500g sugar
1 tablespoon salt
2 cups white vinegar

In a saucepan simmer the pepper and onions in the oil, covered, for 15 minutes. Add the remaining ingredients and cook very slowly for 1 hour or until thickened.
   Allow to cool, then spoon into clean jars and seal.
Makes 3 litres.

Herb Chutney

Here is a way to preserve the unique flavour of fresh herbs. You can make sage and rosemary chutney for pork and chicken, a mint chutney for lamb or a mixed herb chutney to add to casseroles. They all go well with soft and creamy cheeses too.

1.5 kg cooking apples
1 kg onions
250g dried apricots
250g raisins
2 tablespoons grated fresh ginger

300g sugar
2 cups white vinegar
100g fresh mint or *50g mixed fresh sage and rosemary* or *100g*
*   mixed fresh herbs including mint, thyme, tarragon, parsley,*
*   a little sage and a little rosemary*

Peel, core and slice the apples. Finely chop the onions, apricots and raisins, combine with the apples and place in a large saucepan along with the ginger, sugar and vinegar.

Bring the mixture to the boil, stirring occasionally, then cover the saucepan and simmer the chutney over a low heat for about 45 minutes to 1 hour or until the mixture is thickened. Stir occasionally to prevent sticking.

Remove the leaves from the chosen herbs, and chop them finely, discarding the stalks. At the end of cooking time, add the chopped herbs to the chutney, stir well, bring back to the boil, then spoon into hot, clean jars and seal.
Makes about 5 litres.

Indian Chutney

An excellent hot, all-round chutney.

1 kg gooseberry pulp
500g sultanas
500g dates, finely chopped
100g crystallised ginger, finely chopped
6 cloves garlic, finely chopped
2 cups malt vinegar
500g brown sugar
500g white sugar
2 teaspoons cayenne pepper
2 tablespoons salt

Combine all the ingredients in a large saucepan. Bring to the boil and boil for 15 minutes, stirring often.
Pour into hot, clean jars and seal.
Makes about 2 litres.

Kiwifruit Chutney

The distinctive flavour of kiwifruit makes an excellent and versatile chutney.

1 kg kiwifruit
3 onions
2 bananas
1 cup raisins
2 tablespoons chopped crystallised ginger
1 cup brown sugar
2 teaspoons salt
1 teaspoon ground ginger
¼ teaspoon cayenne pepper
juice of 2 lemons
1 cup white wine vinegar

Peel and slice the kiwifruit, finely chop the onions and slice the bananas. Combine with the remaining ingredients in a large saucepan, and bring to the boil, stirring often.

Gently boil for about 1–1½ hours, stirring occasionally, until soft and thick.

Allow to cool, then spoon into clean jars and seal.
Makes about 2 litres.

Kiwifruit and Apple Chutney

Much less sweet than the usual chutney, this is quite sharp and ideal with meats.

500g apples
1 clove garlic
2 tablespoons lemon juice
1 cup brown sugar
1 cup cider vinegar
1 cup sultanas
¼ teaspoon salt
½ teaspoon ground cinnamon

½ teaspoon ground ginger
½ teaspoon ground cumin
750g kiwifruit

Peel, quarter and core the apples and cut them into 1cm cubes. Peel and finely chop the garlic. In a large saucepan combine the apples, garlic, lemon juice, sugar, vinegar, sultanas, salt and spices. Stir together, bring to the boil and boil, uncovered, very gently for 20 minutes, stirring often.

Meanwhile, peel the kiwifruit and cut into 1cm cubes. Add to the apple mixture, bring to the boil and cook very slowly, stirring often, until the chutney is thickened.

Spoon into hot, clean jars and seal.
Makes about 1.5 litres.

Lemon Chutney

The flavour is sharp and great with curries, cheeses or cold chicken or lamb.

7 thin-skinned lemons
1½ tablespoons salt
500g raisins
4 cloves garlic
1 teaspoon chilli powder
1 tablespoon finely grated fresh ginger
1½ cups cider vinegar
500g brown sugar
2 teaspoons grated horseradish

Cut each lemon into 8 pieces and discard the pips. Put in a large bowl, sprinkle with the salt and let stand for 2 days.

Drain and keep the liquid.

Mince the lemons with the raisins and garlic. Place in a large saucepan, add the spices, vinegar and drained liquid, then stir in the sugar and horseradish. Bring to the boil and cook gently, uncovered, until thick.

Pour into hot, clean jars and seal when cold.
Makes about 3 litres.

Lemon and Fig Chutney

Extremely good with cold meat, cheese or curry.

6 large lemons
500g onions
2 tablespoons salt
250g dried figs, finely chopped
500g sugar
2 tablespoons mustard seeds, crushed
¼ teaspoon cayenne pepper
1 teaspoon ground ginger
malt vinegar

Wash the lemons, slice them and remove the pips. Peel and chop the onions finely. Place the onions and lemons in a shallow container, sprinkle with the salt and let stand for 24 hours. Drain off any juices.

Place the lemons and onions in a saucepan with all the other ingredients. Cover with vinegar and simmer for about 2 hours, stirring often, until tender and thick.

Pour into hot, clean jars while hot, and allow to cool before sealing.

Makes about 2 litres.

Lemon and Raisin Chutney

Delicious with cold meats or curries or used as a sandwich spread.

4 medium onions
5 large lemons
1 tablespoon salt
600 ml cider vinegar
1 teaspoon ground allspice
2 tablespoons mustard seed
500g sugar
125g raisins

Peel and slice the onions, and cut the lemons into small pieces, discarding the pips. Combine the onions and lemons in a bowl, sprinkle with the salt and let stand overnight.

Combine all the ingredients in a saucepan, bring to the boil and simmer for about 45 minutes, until the chutney is tender.

Spoon into hot, clean jars and seal when cool.

Lime Chutney

Superb with curries or cold lamb.

6 limes
1 tablespoon salt
1 medium onion, finely chopped
225g sugar
300 ml cider vinegar
1 teaspoon ground mixed spice
2 tablespoons mustard seeds
50g raisins

Chop the limes finely, sprinkle with the salt and let stand for 12 hours.

Place all the ingredients in a saucepan and simmer, covered, for about 45 minutes or until tender and thickened.

Pour into hot, clean jars and seal when cool.

Makes about 1 litre.

Mango Chutney

The classic chutney for curries but it can also be used with cold meats, especially lamb, and with cheese. This delicious version is medium to hot.

1.5 kg raw sugar
6 cups malt vinegar
24 green mangoes
500g raisins or sultanas
125g garlic
250g preserved ginger
25g fresh ginger
12 small dried chillies
2 tablespoons salt

Boil the sugar with half the vinegar until a light syrup is obtained. Peel and slice the mangoes, finely chop the raisins, garlic, preserved ginger, fresh ginger and chillies and add, with the salt, to the syrup. Mix well and slowly stir in the remaining vinegar. Bring to the boil and cook slowly for about 2 hours, until a good colour and consistency are obtained.

   Pour into hot, clean jars and seal.
   Makes about 3.5 litres.

Marrow Chutney

A sort of marrow chow chow with a good strong mustard flavour.

1.5 kg marrow
750g apples
600g onions
250g brown sugar
100g sultanas
4 cups malt vinegar
6 tablespoons mustard
1½ tablespoons turmeric

Peel and marrow, discard the seeds and cut the marrow into small pieces. Peel and core the apples, peel the onions and finely chop them both.

Place the marrow, apples and onions in a saucepan with the sugar, sultanas and 3 cups vinegar, and boil for 20 minutes.

Mix the mustard and turmeric to a paste with the remaining cup of vinegar and stir into the chutney. Boil for a further 10 minutes, stirring often.

Pour into hot, clean jars and seal. When the chutney is cool it is ready to eat.

Makes about 3 litres.

Mint Chutney

Strong and superb, use it sparingly in lamb sandwiches, with barbecued lamb, with lamb burgers or with roast lamb.

250g fresh mint leaves
1 tablespoon salt
½ teaspoon cayenne pepper
125g raisins
50g fresh ginger, sliced
25g garlic, sliced
½ cup brown sugar
1 cup cold malt vinegar
1 cup hot malt vinegar

In the food processor finely chop the mint leaves. Add the dry ingredients until well chopped, then add the cold vinegar and process until smooth.

Alternatively, the solid ingredients can be minced, then pounded to a paste with the cold vinegar.

Put the paste into a bowl and mix in the boiling vinegar. Allow to cool.

Spoon into small, clean jars and seal.

Nectarine Chutney

Absolutely superb, this is all that a fruit chutney should be—spicy, sweet and full of flavour. When peaches are substituted for the nectarines it becomes *Maharajah's Chutney*.

2 kg stoned nectarines
500g onions
100g crystallised ginger
250g preserved mixed peel
500g raisins
500g brown sugar
3 tablespoons salt
1 teaspoon cayenne pepper
1 tablespoon curry powder
3½ cups malt vinegar

Chop the nectarines, onions and ginger. Put into a large saucepan with the rest of the ingredients and mix well. Bring to the boil and cook gently for 1 hour, stirring occasionally.
   Spoon into clean jars when cold, and seal.
   Makes about 4 litres.

Orange Chutney

Excellent with roast lamb or roast duck.

2 large oranges
2 apples
2 large onions
1 cup brown sugar
100g raisins
1 tablespoon ground ginger
1 tablespoon salt
300 ml malt vinegar

Peel the oranges, remove cores and pith and slice finely, discarding any pips. Peel the apples, discard the cores and chop finely. Peel the onions and chop finely.

Put the oranges, apples and onions in a saucepan with the brown sugar, raisins, ginger, salt and vinegar. Bring to the boil and cook very slowly until the fruit is tender.

Spoon into hot, clean jars and seal.

Makes about 1 litre.

Parsnip and Apple Chutney

Swede turnip or carrots can be substituted for the parsnips, or all apples may be used. Instead of lemon juice, vinegar only can be used.

1 kg parsnips
500g onions
1 large clove garlic
1 kg apples
125g pitted dates
250g sultanas
250g sugar
2 teaspoons salt
1 tablespoon ground ginger
1 tablespoon mustard
1 teaspoon cayenne pepper
2½ cups white vinegar
2½ cups lemon juice
1½ tablespoons pickling spice (tied in muslin)

Peel and finely chop the parsnips, onions and garlic. Peel, core and coarsely chop the apples. Finely chop the dates. Combine with the other ingredients in a large saucepan. Cover and simmer very gently for about 2 hours, stirring occasionally. If the chutney dries out too much during cooking, add some more vinegar.

Discard the spice bag, spoon the chutney into hot, clean jars and seal when cold.

Makes about 4 litres.

Passionfruit Chutney

A sweet chutney, excellent with cold meats, especially beef and pork. Banana passionfruit pulp could also be used.

500g passionfruit pulp
1 small onion, chopped
1 cup sultanas
1½ cups white vinegar
2 cups brown sugar
1 tablespoon salt
½ teaspoon dry mustard
½ teaspoon curry powder
¼ teaspoon ground ginger
pinch cayenne pepper

Boil the passionfruit pulp, the onion and the sultanas in the vinegar, uncovered, for 1 hour. Add the remaining ingredients, mix well and gently cook for another 15 minutes.

Allow to cool before spooning into clean jars and seal.
Makes about 1 litre.

Mountain Pawpaw Chutney

Mountain pawpaws are the small yellow, tart pawpaws that grow in New Zealand, as opposed to the large, orange, tropical pawpaw. The pawpaw purée makes a deliciously fruity chutney.

1 kg mountain pawpaws
2 cups white vinegar
500g apples
500g tomatoes
2 cups raisins
2 cloves garlic
1¼ cups sugar
2 teaspoons salt
¼ teaspoon cayenne pepper
1 tablespoon pickling spice

Wash and halve the pawpaws. Scoop out the seeds and chop the flesh finely. Combine the pawpaw seeds, the flesh and 1 tablespoon of the white vinegar in a saucepan and slowly cook the pawpaw until pulpy, taking care it doesn't stick to the pan. Rub the pawpaw through a sieve, producing as much purée as possible.

Peel and core the apples, skin the tomatoes and chop them very finely along with the raisins and garlic. Combine with the pawpaw purée and the remaining ingredients in a pan and simmer very gently, stirring often, until the mixture thickens.

Pour into hot, clean jars and seal.

Makes about 2 litres.

Peach Chutney

This is probably *the* best chutney ever. The longer it is kept the better, as the cayenne pepper mellows and makes the chutney superb.

1 kg stoned and peeled, ripe peaches
3½ cups malt vinegar
2 cloves garlic, finely chopped
100g preserved ginger, finely chopped
500g dates, finely chopped
500g raisins
1 kg brown sugar
2 teaspoons cayenne pepper
2 tablespoons salt

Chop the peaches fairly finely and boil them in the vinegar with the garlic until the peaches are soft. Add the remaining ingredients and boil for 30 minutes, stirring occasionally.

Spoon into hot, clean jars and seal.

Makes about 3 litres.

Indian Peach Chutney

A medium to hot fruit chutney, simply spiced yet strongly flavoured.

3 kg ripe peaches
3 medium onions, finely chopped
50g garlic, crushed
50g fresh ginger, grated or minced
4 chillies, finely chopped
1 kg brown sugar
750g raisins
1 tablespoon ground cinnamon
2 tablespoons salt
1.5 litres malt vinegar

Peel the peaches, chop them and discard the stones.

Combine all the ingredients in a large saucepan. Bring to the boil and cook very slowly for about 1½ hours, or until thickened.

Spoon into hot, clean jars and seal. This chutney is best left several months before using.

Makes about 5 litres.

Peach and Plum Chutney

The fresh chillies and ginger and spices combine with the aromatic fruits to make an excellent chutney.

1 kg peaches
1 kg plums
1 large onion, finely chopped
6 cloves garlic, finely chopped
4 fresh chillies, seeded and finely chopped
4 tablespoons finely chopped fresh ginger
½ cup dates, halved and stoned
½ cup raisins
2 tablespoons brown mustard seeds
1 tablespoon garam masala

1 tablespoon salt
2 cups sugar
2 cups white vinegar

Pour boiling water over the fruit, let stand for several minutes, then peel it. Cut the fruit into small pieces discarding the stones.

Combine all the ingredients in a large saucepan. Bring to the boil and cook very gently, stirring often, for about 30–45 minutes, until the chutney is thick.

Pour into hot, clean jars and seal.
Makes about 3 litres.

Peach and Tomato Chutney

Pleasantly aromatic, this chutney is not very hot so you could add more cayenne pepper if you wish.

2 kg peaches
1 kg tomatoes
1 kg apples
1 kg onions
1 teaspoon cloves
2 tablespoons black peppercorns
1 tablespoon salt
½ teaspoon cayenne pepper
1 kg brown sugar
3 cups malt vinegar

Peel the fruit and vegetables and chop them finely. Tie the cloves and peppercorns in muslin.

Combine all the ingredients in a large saucepan, bring to the boil and cook very gently for about 2½ hours or until the chutney is thick.

Pour into hot, clean jars and seal.
Makes about 4 litres.

Pear Chutney

Another good fruit chutney.

1.5 kg ripe pears
500g pitted dates
25g garlic
500g sultanas
500g sugar
1½ tablespoons salt
½ teaspoon cayenne pepper
5 cups malt vinegar

Remove the cores from the pears and chop the pears into small pieces. Finely chop the dates and crush the garlic. Combine all the ingredients in a large saucepan and boil very gently for about 3 hours, stirring occasionally, until the chutney is thick.

Pour into hot, clean jars and seal.
Makes about 3.5 litres.

Pear and Plum Chutney

Aromatic and spicy.

1 kg pears, cored
1 kg plums, stoned
500g apples, peeled and cored
500g onions, peeled
500g raisins
500g pitted dates
750g treacle
4 tablespoons salt
½ teaspoon cayenne pepper
4 tablespoons ground ginger
2 tablespoons ground allspice
2 litres malt vinegar

Finely chop, or mince, the fruit, the onions and the raisins and dates. Combine all the ingredients in a large saucepan,

bring to the boil, stirring, and cook very gently for about
2 hours, stirring occasionally, until the chutney is thick.
   Pour into hot, clean jars and seal.
Makes about 5 litres.

Pepino Chutney

The perfumed pepinos and the hot ginger make a superb
combination. This chutney is best kept for at least 3 months
to allow the pepino flavour to fully develop and the ginger
to mellow. Apples, chokos, pawpaw, any melon other than
watermelon, or other fruits can be used for this chutney. These
should be peeled first.

2.5 kg pepinos
3 large onions
4½ cups malt vinegar
4 cups sugar
1 tablespoon salt
250g fresh ginger, finely chopped or minced
2 tablespoons cracked black pepper
2 tablespoons mustard seeds

Wash the pepinos and chop them into small pieces, discarding
the seeds. Finely chop the onions. Place the pepinos and onions
in a large saucepan with barely enough water to cover. Bring
to the boil, simmer until just tender, then drain.
   Add the remaining ingredients and boil gently, uncovered,
for 1 hour or until thick.
   Pour into hot, clean jars and seal.
Makes about 3 litres.

Persimmon Chutney

Astringent like most persimmon dishes and a rather strange texture but still great for persimmon lovers.

2 kg ripe persimmons
2 medium onions, finely chopped
2 cloves garlic, finely chopped
1 tablespoon salt
2 cups sugar
½ teaspoon cayenne pepper
2 cups vinegar
1 cup lemon juice
4 teaspoons pickling spice

Remove the stalk end from the persimmons and chop the persimmons very finely, ideally in a food processor. Combine in a large saucepan with the onions, garlic, salt, sugar, cayenne pepper, vinegar and lemon juice.

Tie the pickling spice in muslin and add to the saucepan. Bring to the boil and simmer very gently for 1½–2 hours until the liquid is well reduced.

Allow to cool, then spoon into clean jars and seal.
Makes about 2 litres.

Pineapple Chutney

A mild, sweet chutney, ideal with ham and pork.

1 large fresh pineapple
1 tablespoon salt
1 clove garlic, chopped
1¾ cups raisins
1¼ cups brown sugar
1 cup cider vinegar
2 x 5cm sticks cinnamon
¼ teaspoon ground cloves

Peel, slice and finely chop the pineapple. Sprinkle it with the salt, let stand for 1½ hours, then drain.

Mince or finely chop the garlic and raisins. Combine the sugar, vinegar, cinnamon and cloves in a saucepan and bring to the boil. Stir in the pineapple and the raisin mixture and cook over a low heat for about 45 minutes until thickened.

Ladle into hot, clean jars and seal.

Makes about 1.25 litres.

Plum Chutney

Cold meats, sandwiches and cheeses taste better with this tangy chutney.

1 kg plums
1 cup brown sugar
2 cups malt vinegar
25g garlic
2 tablespoons ground ginger
1 tablespoon salt
2 teaspoons freshly ground black pepper
350g sultanas

Stone the plums and place in a large saucepan with the brown sugar and vinegar. Cook gently for about 30 minutes until the plums are soft.

Add the peeled and chopped garlic, the ground ginger, salt, freshly ground black pepper and sultanas. Boil very gently, stirring occasionally, for about 1 hour, or until the mixture is thick.

Pour into hot, clean jars and seal when cold.

Makes about 1.5 litres.

Prune Chutney

Sweet and spicy with the added flavour of the prune kernels.

1 kg prunes
500g sultanas
50g garlic, finely chopped
500g sugar
4 tablespoons ground ginger
1 tablespoon salt
½ teaspoon cayenne pepper
5 cups malt vinegar

Soak the prunes in cold water for a few hours. Drain, remove and retain the stones and coarsely chop the prunes. Combine the prunes with the other ingredients in a large saucepan. Bring to the boil and cook very slowly for about 1 hour.

Break the stones, add the chopped kernels to the chutney, then spoon into hot, clean jars and seal.
Makes about 1.75 litres.

Pumpkin Chutney

An excellent substitute for mango chutney and great with curries, cheese and meats.

1.5 kg pumpkin
500g ripe tomatoes, peeled and chopped
250g onions, sliced
50g sultanas
1 cup caster sugar
1 cup brown sugar
2 tablespoons salt
2 teaspoons each ground ginger, black pepper and allspice
pinch ground cloves
2 cloves garlic, crushed
½ teaspoon ground mace
2½ cups cider vinegar

Peel the pumpkin, remove seeds, and cut flesh into small chunks. Place all the ingredients in a large, heavy saucepan and bring to the boil, stirring until all the sugar has dissolved. Cook gently, stirring, until the chutney is thick. Take care not to overcook or the pumpkin pieces will lose their shape and become pulpy.

Pour the chutney into hot, clean jars, leave to cool, then seal. Stored in a cool, dark place, it will keep for about 2–3 months.

Makes about 3 litres.

Quince Chutney

Strongly perfumed quinces make a delightful chutney, full-bodied and full of flavour.

6 large quinces
1 kg apples
500g tomatoes
4 large onions
6 chillies
1 kg brown sugar
2 tablespoons salt
2 tablespoons ground ginger
¼ teaspoon cayenne pepper
1 teaspoon mustard
1 teaspoon curry powder
250g raisins
malt vinegar

Peel and core the quinces and apples, peel the tomatoes and onions, seed the chillies and chop all of them finely. Combine with the remaining ingredients in a large saucepan and mix well. Just cover with vinegar.

Boil, uncovered, very slowly for 3 or 4 hours until the chutney is thick.

Pour into hot, clean jars and seal.

Makes about 5 litres.

Quince and Fruit Chutney

Quinces combined with other fruits and flavourings make a very sophisticated and fine chutney.

500g quinces
500g apples
500g tomatoes
400g onions
50g garlic
500g raisins
125g mixed peel
125g crystallised ginger
250g brown sugar
½ teaspoon ground black pepper
½ teaspoon ground cloves
½ teaspoon black pepper
2 tablespoons salt
1 tablespoon ground ginger
3 cups malt vinegar

Peel and core the quinces and apples. Peel the tomatoes, onions and garlic. Mince the quinces, apples, tomatoes, onions, garlic, raisins, mixed peel and crystallised ginger.

Combine all the ingredients in a large saucepan. Bring to the boil and cook very slowly, uncovered, for 1½–2 hours. If the chutney is too thick, add a little more vinegar.

Pour into hot, clean jars and seal.

Makes about 3 litres.

Ratatouille Chutney

Serve this chilli-hot chutney with cold meats, or grilled or barbecued dishes such as hamburgers and steaks.

1 kg ripe tomatoes, skinned and chopped
500g onions, finely chopped
500g eggplant, diced

500g courgettes, sliced
2 large green peppers, seeded and diced
3 cloves garlic, finely chopped
2 teaspoons chilli powder
1 tablespoon salt
1½ cups malt vinegar
500g sugar

Put all the vegetables in a large saucepan. Add the garlic, chilli powder and salt. Heat gently, stirring occasionally, until the juices run from the vegetables, then bring them to the boil. Lower heat and simmer, covered, for about 1 hour until the vegetables are soft, but still in whole pieces, and most of the liquid has evaporated. Add the vinegar and sugar and cook for a further hour until the chutney is thick.

Pour into hot, clean jars and seal. If possible, leave for 2 months before using.

Makes about 2.5 litres.

Rhubarb Chutney

Superbly tangy and not too spicy.

1 kg rhubarb   8 Cup
25g fresh ginger, well bruised – Size of Lemon (med)
25g garlic, finely chopped – Med size Bulb
2 lemons
1 tablespoon salt
2½ cups malt vinegar
1 kg sugar 6 Cups
500g sultanas – 4 Cups

Cut the rhubarb into small pieces. Combine in a saucepan with the ginger, garlic, grated rind and juice of the 2 lemons and the salt. Add the vinegar and slowly bring to the boil, then add the sugar and sultanas. Boil very slowly until the mixture is thick, taking care that it doesn't burn. Remove the ginger.

Allow to cool, then spoon into clean jars and seal.

Makes about 3 litres.

Rhubarb and Orange Chutney

Ideal with cold meats and cheeses and as a sandwich spread.

1 kg rhubarb   8 Cups
2 oranges
2 medium onions
100g raisins – 1½ Cup
2 cups malt vinegar
500g raw sugar   4 Cups
¼ teaspoon brown mustard seeds
½ teaspoon ground coriander   CLOVES
large pinch ground allspice

Wash and trim the rhubarb and cut into 2.5cm lengths. Finely grate the orange rind and squeeze the juice. Finely chop the onions. Combine the rhubarb, orange rind, orange juice, onions, raisins, vinegar and sugar in a large saucepan. Add the spices and slowly bring to the boil, stirring often. Reduce heat and simmer for about 1½ hours, stirring occasionally, until thick and pulpy.
   Pour into hot, clean jars and seal.
Makes about 2 litres.

Ritz Chutney

The chutney of chutneys — if you can get a pie or jam melon. This recipe makes a large amount so can easily be halved. Be warned that chopping the melon into pieces is as time-consuming as peeling pickling onions — but without the tears.

6 kg pie melon (jam melon)
2 tablespoons small dried red chillies
500g pitted dates
250g garlic
500g sultanas
4 kg sugar
100g salt
1.8 litres malt vinegar

Remove the hard skin of the pie melon, discard the seeds, and chop the pie melon into little-finger-nail-sized pieces. Crush the chillies and finely chop the dates and garlic.

Mix all the ingredients together and let stand overnight.

Next day, bring the chutney to the boil and cook gently, uncovered, for about 2 hours, until golden brown.

Pour into hot, clean jars and seal.

Initially the chutney will be very, very liquid. When it has slowly thickened with time, it is ready to eat. This chutney keeps for a long, long time. The more years it is kept the hotter and darker it becomes.

Makes about 9 litres.

Swede Turnip Chutney

An old-fashioned chutney that is especially good with all cold meats.

500g swede turnips
500g onions
1 large apple
1 cup raisins or sultanas
1½ cups sugar
1 teaspoon ground ginger
¼ teaspoon ground cloves
½ teaspoon ground cinnamon
2 teaspoons powdered mustard
1 teaspoon turmeric
3 small chillies, chopped
1 tablespoon golden syrup
1 tablespoon salt
4½ cups malt vinegar

Peel the swede turnips and onions and mince or very finely chop them. Core and finely chop the unpeeled apple.

Combine all the ingredients in a saucepan. Bring to the boil, then simmer slowly, uncovered, for 1 hour.

Pour into hot, clean jars and seal when cold.

Makes about 2 litres.

Tamarillo Chutney

Although this chutney does not use a lot of spice, the taste is still surprisingly good.

24 tamarillos
750g apples
500g onions
600 ml malt vinegar
1 tablespoon salt
1½ teaspoons powdered mustard
1 teaspoon mixed spice
1 kg brown sugar

Peel and chop the tamarillos, core and chop the apples and peel and finely chop the onions.

Combine all the ingredients in a saucepan and simmer very gently, covered, for about 2 hours, stirring often.

Pour into hot, clean jars and seal.

Makes about 2 litres.

Tangelo and Apple Chutney

A sweet and tangy chutney, ideal with cheese or in sandwiches.

2 kg apples
500g raisins
250g walnuts
¼ teaspoon ground cloves
5 cups white vinegar
3 tangelos or *2 oranges*
1 kg sugar

Peel and core the apples, and chop them finely. Chop the raisins and walnuts. Put the apples, raisins, walnuts, ground cloves and vinegar in a saucepan, and simmer, covered, until thoroughly cooked.

Finely grate the rind from the tangelos and squeeze the juice. Add the grated rind, juice and sugar to the saucepan and cook

gently, uncovered, stirring occasionally, until thick.
Pour into hot, clean jars and seal.
Makes about 4 litres.

Tomato Chutney

Use instead of tomato sauce or try it in omelettes or as a sandwich spread. This is made from ripe tomatoes as opposed to green tomatoes.

12 ripe tomatoes (about 2 kg)
3–4 tart green apples, cored and quartered (about 500g)
6 cloves garlic, crushed
3 medium onions, sliced
2½ cups cider vinegar
2⅓ cups brown sugar
1 tablespoon mustard
¼ teaspoon cayenne pepper
2 tablespoons salt
1 tablespoon ground ginger
¼ teaspoon ground cloves
2 bay leaves

Mash the tomatoes with a potato masher or coarsely purée them in a food processor. Combine with the remaining ingredients in a large saucepan and mix well.

Bring to the boil and cook slowly, uncovered, for about 1 hour or until the mixture is soft and pulpy. Let the cooked mixture stand for 2 hours.

The chutney can then be forced through a coarse sieve but better still, remove the bay leaves and coarsely purée the chutney in the food processor.

Pour into clean jars and seal.
Makes about 4 litres.

Tomato and Date Chutney

An excellent hot and spicy all-purpose chutney.

3 kg ripe tomatoes
1 kg pitted dates
250g onions
250g preserved ginger
500g brown sugar
2 tablespoons salt
1 teaspoon cayenne pepper
4 cloves garlic, crushed
2 litres malt vinegar

Peel and slice the tomatoes, and finely chop the dates, onions and ginger.
    Combine all the ingredients in a large saucepan and cook very gently for 3–4 hours, until thickened.
    Pour into hot, clean jars and seal.
    Makes about 5 litres.

Green Tomato Chutney

A sweet and hot-tasting chutney to add 'zing' to cold snacks or to complement curries. Spread it on cheese sandwiches, in hamburgers or serve with a cold meat platter.

2 kg green tomatoes, chopped
500g onions, finely chopped
250g sultanas
3 tablespoons mustard seeds
1 tablespoon ground allspice
1 tablespoon salt
2½ cups white vinegar
500g white sugar

Combine all the ingredients in a large saucepan and bring to the boil, stirring, until the sugar is dissolved. Cook very gently, uncovered, for 1½–2 hours, until the liquid has evaporated and the tomatoes have pulped.

Pour the chutney into hot, clean jars and seal. It is best left for 2 months before using.

Makes about 3.5 litres.

Uncooked Mint Chutney

A delicious chutney with many uses. Try it with cheese in sandwiches or with cold lamb and other meats.

1 cup finely chopped fresh mint
250g apples, peeled, cored and finely chopped
1 cup raisins, finely chopped
3 medium onions, finely chopped
250g tomatoes, peeled and finely chopped
2 cups malt vinegar
2 cups sugar
2 teaspoons mustard powder
2 teaspoons salt
2 teaspoons white pepper

The mint, apples, raisins and onions can be finely chopped in the food processor. The tomatoes should be chopped by hand. Combine them all in a large bowl.

In a saucepan bring to the boil the vinegar, sugar, mustard, salt and white pepper, stirring until the sugar is dissolved. Boil for 3 minutes, then remove from heat and allow to cool. When cold stir into the mint mixture and combine the ingredients well.

Spoon into clean jars and seal.

Makes about 2.5 litres.

Uncooked Chilli Chutney

A clean-tasting, zesty chutney, excellent with cold roast beef or lamb.

3 long red chilli peppers
500g peeled and cored cooking apples
500g onions
1½ teaspoons salt
5 tablespoons sugar
1 cup white vinegar

Split the chillies lengthwise and remove and discard the seeds. Mince together the chillies, apples and onions, or chop them very finely in the food processor.

Sprinkle with the salt and sugar, then add the vinegar, mix thoroughly and let stand for 8 hours.

Mix again, then spoon into clean jars and seal.
Makes about 1.5 litres.

Uncooked Date and Apple Chutney

A marvellous recipe to use when you run out of chutney or need some in a hurry, because this is ready as soon as it is made. Use it for all the normal uses for chutney and try it with fried or grilled fish too.

500g stoned dates
500g onions
500g apples, peeled and cored
500g brown sugar
½ teaspoon salt
pepper
1 teaspoon mustard
2½ cups malt vinegar

Mince together the dates, onions and apples. In a bowl combine all the ingredients and let stand overnight, stirring occasionally.

Next day, spoon into clean jars and seal.

The Relishes

The term 'relish' can be used to describe any vegetable chutney—but it is also the all-embracing name for pickles, chutneys and the like. So, because things tend to get mixed up when you try to sort out exact categories, the definition of a relish here is a preserve made from finely chopped fresh vegetables or fruits, pickled in a lightly spiced syrup of sugar and vinegar.

Normally a relish is less spiced than a chutney and does not contain dried fruit, as many chutneys do.

Relishes are able to be used almost immediately after making and are invariably excellent meat accompaniments, going well with cheese, especially in sandwiches. They are great with hamburgers and hot dogs and are also excellent by themselves. An exception to all this is the fiery chilli relish, but then there is always an exception or two to the rule.

Relishes are not cooked for long, so that the ingredients still have some crunch, as in many pickles. In fact, another definition of a relish might be a finely chopped pickle. Generally, relishes do not keep as long as pickles, and rarely improve with age.

Barbecue Relish

It is just what it says, a barbecue relish. Marvellous to serve at barbecues with all barbecue meats. Or try this relish in cold meat sandwiches, especially with roast beef.

1 kg cucumbers, peeled, seeded and finely chopped
1 kg onions, finely chopped
1 kg green tomatoes, finely chopped
3 red peppers, seeded and finely chopped
1 green pepper, seeded and finely chopped
½ cup salt
1½ cups sugar
4 cups white vinegar
½ cup mixed pickling spices (tied in muslin)
½ teaspoon cayenne pepper

Place the prepared vegetables in a large bowl. Sprinkle with the salt and toss to mix well. Cover and let stand overnight.

Next day, drain the liquid from the vegetables and rinse them well.

Combine the sugar, vinegar and spices in a large saucepan. Heat, stirring, until the sugar dissolves. Add the vegetables, heat to boiling, then cook gently for 45 minutes. Discard the spice bag. Spoon the mixture into hot, clean jars and seal.

Makes about 3.5 litres.

Bean Relish

Tender runner beans are ideal for this relish to be served with cold meats or as a salad.

2 kg sliced green beans
6 large onions, halved and finely sliced
2 tablespoons salt
2 teaspoons turmeric
1 tablespoon dry mustard
2 teaspoons white pepper

750g sugar
5 cups malt vinegar
2 cups water
2 tablespoons flour

Place all the ingredients, except the flour, in a large saucepan. Bring to the boil and boil, uncovered, until the vegetables are tender.

Mix the flour with a little extra vinegar and stir into the chutney. Cook for a few minutes longer, then spoon into hot, clean jars and seal.

Makes about 4 litres.

Beetroot Relish

Marvellous spread on thin brown bread or cracker biscuits, or served with cold meats.

1 kg beetroot
500g onions
malt vinegar
700g sugar
1 teaspoon salt
1 tablespoon pickling spice (tied in muslin)
2 tablespoons cornflour

Grate or mince the peeled beetroot and onions. Place in a large saucepan, cover with vinegar, then add the sugar, salt and spice. Boil for about 30 minutes, until the beetroot is cooked.

Remove and discard the pickling spice. Mix the cornflour with a little vinegar and stir into the relish. Bring back to the boil and cook for a further few minutes.

Spoon into hot, clean jars and seal.

Makes about 3 litres.

Cabbage and Carrot Relish

This can also be made into a refrigerator pickle by spooning the mixed, raw vegetables into clean jars and pouring over the hot vinegar mixture, cover and refrigerate for several days. Either way, the relish is good with all meats.

4 cups chopped cabbage
3 cups peeled and chopped carrots
5 cups chopped green or red peppers, or a mixture of both
2 cups chopped onions
3½ cups white or cider vinegar
1¼ cups sugar
3 tablespoons salt
2 tablespoons celery seed
1 tablespoon mustard seed

Mix all the vegetables together well. Boil the vinegar, sugar, salt, celery seed and mustard seed together for 2–3 minutes. Add the vegetables, bring to the boil, and cook for 1 minute.
   Spoon into hot, clean jars and seal at once.
Makes about 3.5 litres.

Celery Relish

Also known as *Gazpacho Relish*, this is excellent for hot dogs and hamburgers, as well as cold meats.

1 head celery
2 green peppers, seeded
1 onion
3 cups tomato pulp
1 tablespoon salt
3 tablespoons sugar
¼ teaspoon ground allspice
⅛ teaspoon cayenne pepper
3 cups white vinegar

Finely chop or mince the celery, green peppers and onion.

Combine with the tomato pulp and the other ingredients in a large saucepan and boil gently for about 1½ hours until the vegetables are soft and the relish is thick.

Pour into hot, clean jars and seal.

Makes about 3 litres.

To make tomato pulp: Peel and remove the cores from ripe tomatoes. Chop the tomatoes coarsely and slowly bring to the boil in a saucepan, then cook for a few minutes until a thick pulp is obtained.

Chilli Relish

A red-hot relish to add a little fire to hot or cold meats. This should make just enough to keep you in chilli relish until the next time chillies are available.

1 cup finely sliced green or red chilli peppers
malt vinegar
3 tablespoons sugar
1 tablespoon worcestershire sauce

Place the finely sliced chillies in a small jar with a screw-top lid. Three-quarters cover the chillies with malt vinegar. Add the sugar and place the jar in a saucepan of cold water, deep enough so that the water comes up to the top of the jar's contents. Very slowly heat the water until boiling.

Remove the jar and stir the worcestershire sauce into the relish. Put the top on the jar when it is cold. It is now ready to use.

Corn Relish

Bright and colourful and the perfect accompaniment to cold meats, grills and barbecues.

5 cups whole kernel corn
1 cup chopped green pepper
1 cup chopped red pepper
1 cup chopped celery
½ cup chopped onion
½ cup sugar
3 ¼ cups cider vinegar
2 teaspoons salt
1 teaspoon celery seed
2 teaspoons dry mustard
½ teaspoon turmeric
¼ cup flour
½ cup water

Place corn, peppers, celery, onion, sugar, vinegar, salt and celery seed in a saucepan. Bring to the boil and simmer for about 20 minutes or until the vegetables are just tender.

Mix the mustard, turmeric, flour and water together. Stir into the saucepan, bring back to the boil and simmer for a further 10 minutes, stirring occasionally.

Pour into hot, clean jars and seal.
Makes about 2 litres.

Corn and Cabbage Relish

Pleasantly hot and deliciously corny.

9 cups whole kernel corn (either fresh, frozen or canned)
2 cups finely chopped cabbage
1½ cups finely chopped onion
2 cups finely chopped green peppers
½ cup finely chopped red pepper
1 teaspoon crushed, dried red chillies

2 teaspoons celery seeds
1 teaspoon mustard seeds
2 teaspoons turmeric
2½ tablespoons salt
1 cup sugar
2 cups cider vinegar

Bring the vegetables, spices, salt, sugar and vinegar to the boil in a large saucepan. Cook, uncovered, for 20 minutes, or until the relish is thickened.

Ladle into hot, clean jars and seal at once. Let stand for six weeks before using.

Makes about 3 litres.

Cucumber Relish

Ideal with cold meats and cheeses or as a sandwich filling.

500g peeled, cored apples
2 cups malt vinegar
500g sugar
1 teaspoon white pepper
2 teaspoons curry powder
2 tablespoons turmeric
1 tablespoon salt
500g onions, minced
750g cucumbers

Mince the apples and cook them in the vinegar for about 5 minutes. Add the sugar, pepper, curry powder, turmeric, salt and minced onions. Boil until the onions are soft.

Peel and mince the cucumbers. Add to the relish and boil for a further 5 minutes.

Pour the relish into hot, clean jars and seal.

Makes about 3 litres.

Cucumber and Red Pepper Relish

A sweet, festive-looking pickle which is ideal with cold leftovers at Christmas or in sandwiches, with cold meats or on cracker biscuits all year round.

8 cups finely diced, unpeeled cucumber
4 tablespoons salt
4 onions, finely diced
3 red peppers, finely diced
3 cups sugar
2 cups white vinegar
1 teaspoon celery seed
1 teaspoon mustard seed
pinch cayenne pepper
3 tablespoons cornflour

Before dicing the unpeeled cucumber, discard the seeds. Put the cucumber in a basin, sprinkle with the salt, barely cover with cold water and let stand overnight.

Drain and rinse the cucumber. Put it in a large saucepan with all the other ingredients, except the cornflour, and bring to the boil, stirring constantly. Mix the cornflour with a little water and stir into the relish. Simmer for several minutes, then pour into hot, clean jars and seal.

Makes about 3 litres.

Feijoa Relish

This is lightly spiced and perfumed, and ideal as an all-purpose relish. It should be fairly liquid.

500g feijoas
250g apples
250g onions
1 cup malt vinegar
1 tablespoon ground mixed spice
2 teaspoons salt

½ teaspoon cayenne pepper
2 cups brown sugar

Peel and finely chop the feijoas. Peel, core and finely chop the apples, and peel and chop the onions.

Combine them with the vinegar in a saucepan, bring to the boil and simmer, covered, for 30 minutes. Add the remaining ingredients, bring back to the boil and cook for 5 minutes, stirring often.

Pour into hot, clean jars and seal.
Makes about 3 litres.

Pea Relish

Peas preserved in a good, thick curry-flavoured sauce make an ideal relish to go with cold lamb and other cold meats.

8 cups cooked peas
½ cup flour
2 cups sugar
2 tablespoons curry powder
1 tablespoon mustard
pinch salt
2½ cups malt vinegar

Cook the peas. Mix the dry ingredients with the vinegar in a saucepan, bring to the boil, stirring, and cook for a few minutes until smooth and thick.

Add the peas and slowly bring back to the boil. Pour into hot, clean jars and seal.
Makes about 2 litres.

Pear and Tomato Relish

The combination of tomatoes, pears and green pepper makes a fascinating and delicious all-purpose relish.

500g pears, peeled and finely chopped
500g tomatoes, peeled and chopped
½ cup finely chopped green pepper
¼ cup finely chopped red pepper
½ cup finely chopped onion
1 cup sugar
½ cup malt vinegar
1 teaspoon salt
½ teaspoon ground ginger
½ teaspoon dry mustard
⅛ teaspoon cayenne pepper

Combine all the ingredients in a saucepan, bring to the boil and cook, uncovered, very slowly for about 1 hour or until the relish is reasonably thick.

Pour into clean, hot jars and seal.
Makes about 1 litre.

Note that this can also be puréed in a blender or food processor and used as a thick sauce.

Pepper Relish

Use a mixture of red and green peppers for a colourful relish.

1 kg green and red peppers
500g onions
1 tablespoon salt
2½ cups white sugar
2½ cups white vinegar

Remove the cores and seeds from the peppers and peel the onions. Mince them, then place in a container and sprinkle with the salt. Let stand for 2 hours, then strain off the juices.

In a saucepan combine the strained vegetables with the sugar and vinegar, then gently simmer, uncovered, for 45 minutes or until thick.

Pour into hot, clean jars and seal.

Pineapple Relish

Serve this curry-flavoured relish with cold pork or ham or with cheese sandwiches.

1 large pineapple
1 cup brown sugar
2 tablespoons butter
2 tablespoons cider vinegar
1 teaspoon curry powder
½ teaspoon salt
¼ teaspoon ground ginger

Peel and core the pineapple. Cut into very small pieces. Place in a large saucepan and barely cover with water. Bring to the boil and simmer for 10 minutes.

Drain all the water from the saucepan. Add the remaining ingredients. Bring to the boil, stirring constantly, then simmer, stirring often, for 10 minutes.

Spoon into hot, clean jars and seal.

Makes about 1 litre.

Redcurrant Relish

Here is a relish that when eaten in small quantities turns cold roast lamb into a feast. Use it to add 'zing' to grilled lamb or barbecued lamb. Blackcurrants can be substituted for the redcurrants.

1 kg redcurrants
1 kg onions
4 cloves garlic, crushed
50g fresh ginger, grated
1 teaspoon turmeric
1 teaspoon salt
1 teaspoon ground cardamom
250g brown sugar
1 cup wine vinegar

Top and tail the redcurrants, whether fresh or frozen. Finely chop the onions and place them in a large saucepan with the redcurrants. Add the garlic, grated ginger, turmeric, salt, cardamom and sugar.

Pour in the vinegar, mix well and bring to the boil. Reduce the heat and gently cook the relish, covered, for about 1 hour. Stir frequently during cooking to prevent sticking to the saucepan.

At the end of cooking time the fruit should be soft and pulpy and the juices thickened. Pour into hot, clean jars and seal. Ready for use in 2 weeks.

Makes about 2 litres.

Rhubarb Relish

Good with any cold meats or cheeses.

2 cups finely sliced rhubarb
2 cups halved and finely sliced onions
1 cup malt vinegar
2 cups brown sugar

1½ teaspoons salt
¼ teaspoon ground ginger
¼ teaspoon ground cinnamon
⅛ teaspoon cayenne pepper

Combine all the ingredients in a large saucepan. Bring to the boil and cook slowly, uncovered, for about 20–30 minutes, until the mixture is almost jam consistency.

Pour into hot, clean jars and seal.

Makes about 1 litre.

Tomato Relish

Tomato relish goes with almost everything but is especially good with grilled or barbecued meats, especially hamburgers.

2 kg large ripe tomatoes, peeled and sliced
750g onions, peeled and sliced
salt
12 small dried red chilli peppers, crushed
2 cups malt vinegar
2¼ cups brown sugar
1 tablespoon curry powder
1½ teaspoons mustard
1 tablespoon flour

Layer the tomato and onion slices in a large bowl. Sprinkle with a little salt and let stand overnight.

Next day, drain and place the vegetables in a saucepan with the chilli peppers and 1½ cups vinegar. Heat to boiling and boil for 5 minutes.

Mix the sugar, curry powder, mustard and flour in a bowl. Stir in the remaining ½ cup vinegar to make a smooth paste. Stir the paste into the vegetables. Cook slowly, stirring often, for 1 hour.

Spoon into hot, clean jars and seal.

Makes about 2 litres.

The Sauces and the Ketchups

'Sauce', 'ketchup', 'catchup' and 'catsup' in New Zealand and Australia all mean the same thing: a thick or flowing liquid which adds piquancy, flavour and moisture to otherwise dryish and dullish food. Sausages, chops, cutlets, steaks, cold meats, vegetables, fish, cold chicken, a multitude of dishes, can all be enhanced by a spicy sauce. Tomato sauce is universal: what would a sausage, or baked beans, be without tomato sauce? But how much better they are when the tomato sauce is home-made and not full of unnatural preservatives and additives. Another famous sauce is worcestershire sauce, extremely pungent and with a fascinating history, too.

Most sauces are based on fruit, though there are exceptions. They can be as thin as worcestershire sauce or as thick as chutney. Most are pouring sauces, though a few need to be spooned.

'Ketchup', a word often used instead of sauce, has an equivalent, 'catchup' or 'catsup', which is still used in the United States, while the word 'sauce' there tends to mean a purée. The word 'ketchup' more than likely comes from the old Chinese word *ke-tsiap* which means a fish brine. Today it can mean any sauce, though it originally meant a somewhat salty extract of fish, mushrooms or walnuts, used as a flavouring in dishes rather than as a sauce served with them. One used to think of a thin sauce when one heard the term 'ketchup' — until the advent years ago of the very thin worcestershire *sauce*!

A very smooth sauce is obtained by pushing the mixture through a fine sieve. But when you are making some of these recipes, instead of rubbing the sauce through a sieve, you can purée it in a blender. In this case whole spices should be tied in muslin during the cooking, so they can be discarded before blending, and tough skins and pips or stones should be removed before cooking.

Another way, although the sauce is not quite as smooth, is to put the sauce through a large food mill or mouli. This holds back the tough skins and seeds but pushes through the pulp far more easily than using a sieve.

To prevent discolouring in the tops of sauce bottles, invert the bottles for several minutes while the sauce is still hot, to sterilise the necks of the bottles.

Most sauces are best kept for several months before using, to allow the vinegar flavour to mellow and let the basic flavour predominate.

Some of the sauces in this section can be used in stews, casseroles and soups, to add flavour.

And some of these sauces can be used to colour — and flavour — white sauces, gravies and salad dressings, including mayonnaise.

Apple Ketchup

The quality of this sauce will depend on the apples — the tarter the apple the better, but it will still be good made with any apples. It is piquant and spicy and ideal with hot or cold pork, pork sausages or ham.

4 kg apples
6 large onions
4 tablespoons whole cloves
4 tablespoons whole allspice
½ teaspoon cayenne pepper
2 kg sugar
5 tablespoons salt
2.5 litres malt vinegar

Chop the apples, skin, pips and all. Chop the onions. Tie the whole spices in muslin. Combine all the ingredients in a large saucepan. Bring to the boil, stirring to dissolve the sugar, then simmer, covered, for 1–1½ hours until the fruit is well pulped.

Push the sauce through a sieve or put it through a mouli. Pour the sauce into hot, clean bottles and seal.

Makes about 5 litres.

Apple and Garlic Ketchup

Terrific with hot dogs, saveloys and sausages, especially bratwurst. Shake the bottle well before using.

750g apples
250g garlic
1.5 litres malt vinegar
piece root ginger, bruised
3 chillies, split
2 tablespoons whole cloves
4 teaspoons salt
4 tablespoons peppercorns
500g treacle

Coarsely chop the apples, skins and cores included. Do not peel the garlic but separate the cloves.

Combine all the ingredients, except the treacle, in a large saucepan and boil very gently for about 1 hour, until the apples have pulped and the garlic is very tender. Rub through a strainer and return the sauce to the cleaned saucepan.

Add the treacle and bring to the boil, then boil for a further 5 minutes.

Pour into hot, clean bottles and seal. Should be kept for several months before using.

Makes about 2 litres.

Apricot Sauce

A deliciously fruity sauce, ideal with any meats or cheese dishes.

3 kg apricots, stoned and chopped
1 kg onions, finely chopped
4 large apples, chopped
6 teaspoons salt
1 kg brown sugar
7 cups malt vinegar
3 tablespoons whole cloves
3 tablespoons whole allspice
3 tablespoons black peppercorns
1 teaspoon cayenne pepper

Combine all the ingredients in a large saucepan. Boil very gently for 3 hours, stirring often towards the end of the cooking time. Strain through a sieve, pushing as much through as possible.

Alternatively, tie the spices in muslin. When the mixture is cooked, discard the spices and purée the sauce in a blender or food processor. This will make a thicker sauce.

Pour into hot, clean bottles and seal.

Makes about 4 litres.

Babaco Sauce

It may smell like roast lamb when it is cooking but its taste is fruity and spicy. The equivalent volume of mountain pawpaws or tropical pawpaws can be substituted but if so, use some of the seeds too.

3 medium babacos, roughly chopped
500g sugar
4 tablespoons salt
2 cups lemon juice or lime juice
8 cups malt vinegar
500g onions, minced
125g garlic, minced
125g fresh ginger, minced
3 tablespoons mustard seeds
2 tablespoons pickling spice
12 small hot chillies

In a large saucepan cook all the ingredients together, except the chillies, for 2 hours, partially covered. Half an hour before end of cooking time, add the chopped chillies.

Rub as much as possible through a sieve, add more salt if necessary, and pour into hot, clean bottles and seal.

Makes about 3 litres.

Blackberry Ketchup

A sweetish, gently spiced sauce excellent with meats, but try it with offal too. Boysenberries can be substituted for the blackberries. This is a two-in-one recipe as the leftover pulp can be made into a successful relish.

2 kg ripe blackberries
750g apples
5 cups sugar
¾ teaspoon white pepper
2 teaspoons ground mixed spice

2 teaspoons ground cloves
2 teaspoons salt
2 teaspoons ground ginger
3½ cups white vinegar

Wash the blackberries, and drain well. Core and chop the unpeeled apples. Combine all the ingredients in a large saucepan, bring to the boil, stirring to dissolve the sugar, then cook slowly, uncovered, for about 1½ hours.

Rub as much of the sauce as possible through a fine sieve, reserving the resulting pulp, and pour the sauce into hot, clean bottles.

Makes about 2.5 litres.

The resulting pulp can now be made into a successful relish.

Blackberry Relish

pulp leftover from Blackberry Ketchup
5 medium onions, halved and finely sliced
¾ cup sugar
1 cup malt vinegar
1 teaspoon salt
1 teaspoon mustard
1 teaspoon turmeric
1 teaspoon ground mixed spice
1 teaspoon curry powder

Combine all the ingredients in a saucepan and simmer very gently, partially covered, for 45 minutes, stirring often.

Spoon into small, hot, clean jars and seal.

Makes about 1.5 litres.

Blackcurrant Sauce

Delicious with cold meats or cold chicken, or heated and served with liver or grilled or fried chicken or fish, or with game.

4 cups blackcurrant juice
3 cups white vinegar
750g sugar
1½ teaspoons salt
½ teaspoon ground cloves
½ teaspoon ground allspice
½ teaspoon ground cinnamon
pinch cayenne pepper

Make the juice by boiling blackcurrants with a little water, then rubbing as much as possible through a fine sieve.

Combine the blackcurrant juice with the remaining ingredients. Bring to the boil and cook, uncovered, for 30 minutes.

Pour into hot, clean bottles and seal.
Makes about 1 litre.

Note: The amount of spices is pleasantly light but more could be added if you wish. If the sauce is boiled longer to the jelly stage, this makes a very good, lightly spiced jelly for meats and game.

Blueberry Sauce

A thick, spooning sauce, great with pork sausages, chicken or even over ice-cream.

500g fresh or frozen blueberries
250g sugar
½ cup red wine vinegar
½ teaspoon ground cloves
½ teaspoon ground cinnamon
¼ teaspoon ground allspice

Place all the ingredients in a saucepan. Bring slowly to the boil and cook very gently for 10 minutes, stirring occasionally.

Let stand for 30 minutes, then purée the sauce in the blender. Spoon into small, warmed jars and seal.

Makes about 1 litre.

Chilli Sauce

Not too hot but quite hot enough. After all, what would chilli sauce be if it didn't have *some* fire.

1.5 kg ripe tomatoes
2 medium onions
3 large red peppers
2 teaspoons dried, small red chillies
1 tablespoon salt
½ cup brown sugar
½ teaspoon ground cinnamon
½ teaspoon ground ginger
½ teaspoon ground allspice
2 cups white vinegar

Peel and finely chop the tomatoes and onions, finely chop the red peppers and chillies. Combine all the ingredients in a large saucepan, bring to the boil and cook very gently for about 2 hours.

Purée the mixture in a blender or put it through a food mill. Reheat the sauce and boil for a few minutes to blend, then pour it into hot, clean bottles and seal.

Makes about 2 litres.

Feijoa Sauce

An excellent fruity sauce for all cold meats or pies.

1.5 kg feijoas
2 apples
1 large onion
2 cups brown sugar
1½ teaspoons salt
¼ teaspoon cayenne pepper
1 teaspoon ground cloves
2 teaspoons ground ginger
3 cups malt vinegar

Peel and chop the feijoas. Peel, core and chop the apples and finely chop the onion. Combine all the ingredients in a saucepan and cook very gently, uncovered, for 2–2½ hours.

Process the sauce in a food processor or blender until it is fairly smooth. This is easier than pushing it through a sieve and it does make a much thicker and richer sauce.

Makes about 1.5 litres.

Garlic Sauce

A perfect sauce that, like worcestershire sauce, is thin yet extremely potent. Use for adding interest to casseroles and stews, meat pies and meat loaves. Excellent as a dipping sauce for fish or for such foods as Chinese Dim Sum or spring rolls.

1 large onion
150g garlic
2 tablespoons whole cloves
1½ teaspoons ground ginger
1 tablespoon salt
250g brown sugar
1 kg treacle
5 cups malt vinegar
½ cup worcestershire sauce

Mince the peeled onion and the unpeeled garlic and combine with the remaining ingredients, except the worcestershire sauce, then let stand overnight.

Next day, slowly bring the mixture to the boil and cook gently, uncovered, for 1 hour, stirring occasionally.

Rub the sauce through a sieve, then add the worcestershire sauce and pour the sauce into hot, clean bottles and seal.

Makes about 2 litres.

Gooseberry Catchup

A dark and mysterious sauce, though the ingredients and preparation are comparatively simple. Especially good with cold meat.

1 kg gooseberries
2 cups malt vinegar
1.5 kg brown sugar
¼ teaspoon cayenne pepper
1 tablespoon ground cinnamon
1 tablespoon ground cloves
1 tablespoon ground allspice

Top and tail the gooseberries. (If fresh gooseberries aren't available, frozen ones are excellent value.) Wash and drain them.

Combine the gooseberries with the remaining ingredients in a saucepan. Bring to the boil and simmer very slowly for 30 minutes, stirring occasionally.

In a blender, purée the sauce in batches and pour it into hot, clean bottles. When cold it should be a good thickish consistency. Seal the bottles.

Makes about 1.5 litres.

Grape Ketchup

Aromatic grapes and spices combine well to make a superb sauce for fish, poultry and cheese.

2 kg grapes
2½ cups white vinegar
500g sugar
2 teaspoons salt
1 teaspoon ground cloves
1 teaspoon allspice
1 teaspoon ground cinnamon
¼ teaspoon cayenne pepper

Wash grapes and discard stalks. Place the grapes in a saucepan with the vinegar and boil for 20 minutes. Rub through a fine sieve and return the pulp to a clean saucepan.

Boil the pulp until fairly thick, then add the remaining ingredients and boil for a further 30 minutes.

Fill hot, clean bottles with the ketchup and seal.

Makes about 1.5 litres.

Kiwifruit Sauce

A gorgeous chartreuse colour, this is a spicy sauce, excellent as a general purpose fruit sauce. Note that the riper the fruit the better. Heat this sauce and serve with chicken or fish.

1.5 kg ripe kiwifruit
2 cups white sugar
2 cups white vinegar
½ teaspoon cayenne pepper
1 teaspoon whole cloves
1 teaspoon whole black peppercorns
1 teaspoon ground ginger
2 tablespoons peeled and finely chopped garlic

Peel and mash the kiwifruit. Combine all the ingredients in a large saucepan, bring to the boil and simmer very gently, uncovered, for 1 hour.

Strain as much as possible through a sieve. The more pulp you can push through the sieve, the thicker the sauce. Pour into small bottles and seal.
Makes about 5 cups.

Loquat Sauce

An unusual sauce because of the mixture of spices and flavourings it uses. Any kind of fruit could be used instead of the loquats and the type of fruit used will determine the thickness or thinness of the sauce. Use it as a barbecue sauce or barbecue basting sauce.

2 kg loquats
6½ cups malt vinegar
2 cloves garlic, finely chopped
250g onions, finely chopped
3 cups brown sugar
4 tablespoons treacle
1 tablespoon curry powder
1 tablespoon flour
2 teaspoons dry mustard
1 teaspoon ground cinnamon
1½ teaspoons ground ginger
1½ teaspoons ground mixed spice
½ teaspoon celery seed
1 tablespoon salt

In a large saucepan combine the loquats with 6 cups malt vinegar, the garlic and onions. Boil until the fruit is very soft, then push as much as possible through a fine sieve to remove seeds and skins.

Return the liquid to the cleaned saucepan and bring to the boil. Add the sugar and treacle, stirring until dissolved, then bring back to the boil. Combine the remaining ingredients and mix to a smooth paste with the extra ½ cup vinegar. Slowly stir into the saucepan, then boil for 15 minutes.

Pour into hot, clean bottles and seal.
Makes about 2 litres.

Mango Sauce

This sweetish sauce almost tastes like the traditional mango chutney. It is quite superb with just about everything.

3 kg under-ripe mangoes
1.5 kg white sugar
7 cups malt vinegar
1 teaspoon cayenne pepper
1 teaspoon salt
2 tablespoons whole allspice
1 tablespoon whole cloves
50g fresh ginger, bruised
6 cloves garlic, chopped

Peel and coarsely chop the mangoes. Combine all the ingredients in a large saucepan. Bring to the boil and cook very slowly for about 1½–2 hours, until thickening or until the stones separate. Rub as much as possible through a fine sieve.

Pour into hot, clean bottles and seal.

Makes about 3.5 litres.

Mint Sauce

Make a supply while mint is at its best and it'll save you making it all year round. As well as with the proverbial sheep's meat this sweet mint sauce is excellent in green salad dressings too. You may have to dilute the sauce with a little hot water or vinegar before using.

1 cup finely chopped mint
250g sugar
½ cup malt vinegar
½ cup water
salt and white pepper

Prepare the mint. In the meantime, bring the sugar, vinegar and water to the boil and cook, uncovered, for 5 minutes. Allow to cool.

When the liquid is cold, add the mint and season to taste with salt and white pepper.

Spoon into small bottles or jars and seal.

Mushroom Ketchup

This makes a well-flavoured ketchup, great for seasoning casseroles, meat pies, meat loaves and for making delicious gravies. It is good with cold meats too. Note that if you have a surplus of mushrooms, use more juice and less vinegar.

1 kg flat mushrooms
1 tablespoon salt
4 cups malt vinegar
2 tablespoons whole black peppercorns
2 tablespoons whole allspice
1 tablespoon grated fresh ginger
1 teaspoon ground mace
1 teaspoon whole cloves
pinch cayenne pepper

Slice the mushrooms, place them in a large saucepan, sprinkle with the salt and let stand in a warm place for 24 hours, covered with a damp cloth.

Next day, add the vinegar and slowly bring to the boil, then cover and simmer for 30–40 minutes. Allow to cool enough to strain through muslin, squeezing out as much juice as possible. Return the liquid to the cleaned saucepan.

Tie the spices in muslin and add to the saucepan. Bring to the boil and simmer, covered, for 15 minutes. Allow to cool. Repeat twice more. The more the repeated boiling the better the ketchup. The boiling can be repeated as many as six times, if you have the time and patience.

Remove the spice bag and pour the ketchup into hot, clean bottles and seal.

Makes about 1 litre.

Mustard Sauce

A good, thick spooning sauce for fried fish, smoked fish, hot tongue, or with hot dogs or hamburgers.

1 cup sugar
4 tablespoons dry mustard
2 tablespoons flour
1 cup white vinegar
2 egg yolks, beaten
2 cups cream
1 clove garlic, crushed
salt

Mix the sugar, dry mustard and flour. Stir in the vinegar to make a paste. Turn into the top of a double boiler.

Blend the egg yolks into the cream and add to the paste in the double boiler. Cook over simmering water, stirring often, for about 1 hour, until thick. Strain. Add the garlic and salt to taste.

Seal in hot, clean jars. Keep in the refrigerator after the jar is opened.

Makes about 2 cups.

Passionfruit Ketchup

A sweet ketchup that goes well with cold lamb or beef or with cheese dishes. Banana passionfruit can be used instead of the passionfruit.

500g passionfruit pulp
500g apples
250g onions
2 cups malt vinegar
4 cups brown sugar
1 teaspoon mace
1 teaspoon ground allspice
½ teaspoon ground black pepper

1 tablespoon salt
¼ teaspoon cayenne pepper

Place the passionfruit pulp in a saucepan. Chop the unpeeled apples and peeled onions and add to the saucepan. Stir in the vinegar, bring to the boil and cook, partially covered, for 15 minutes.

Add the remaining ingredients and continue cooking, partially covered, for 30 minutes. Push through a sieve or put through a mouli.

Allow the sauce to cool, then pour into clean bottles and seal.
Makes about 1.5 litres.

Mountain Pawpaw Sauce

The small tart mountain pawpaw makes a superbly fruity sauce.

1 kg mountain pawpaws
2 apples
2 onions
1 cup brown sugar
1 tablespoon salt
1½ teaspoons whole cloves
1 teaspoon ground ginger
4 cloves garlic, chopped
3 chillies, chopped
1 tablespoon mustard seeds
1½ cups malt vinegar
1 cup lemon juice

Chop the pawpaws, unpeeled apples and peeled onions. Combine with the remaining ingredients in a saucepan. Include the pawpaw seeds.

Simmer very slowly for about 2 hours until very pulpy. Rub through a sieve, producing as much sauce as possible.

Reheat, then bottle and seal.
Makes about 1.5 litres.

Pepino Sauce

Perfumed pepinos and strong spices combine to make an unusually good fruit sauce.

1 kg ripe pepinos
4 cups brown sugar
3 cups cider vinegar
1 tablespoon ground cloves
1 tablespoon ground cinnamon
1 tablespoon ground allspice
1 teaspoon salt
½ teaspoon cayenne pepper

Wash and coarsely chop the pepinos. Combine all the ingredients in a large saucepan. Bring to the boil and cook very gently for 1 hour, stirring often.

Purée the sauce in a blender in batches. Mix the sauce well before pouring into hot, clean bottles and seal.
Makes about 2 litres.

Plum Sauce

Sparkle up drab cold meat, dreary sandwiches, plain meat dishes or ordinary cheese with this spicy sauce. Serve it with curries too.

3 kg plums
2 onions
3 cloves garlic
1.5 kg sugar
6 cups malt vinegar
2 tablespoons salt
1 teaspoon cayenne pepper
2 teaspoons ground cloves
2 teaspoons ground ginger
2 teaspoons freshly ground black pepper

Count and note the number of plums. Coarsely chop the onions and crush the garlic. Combine all the ingredients in a large saucepan and bring them to the boil. Cook slowly, uncovered, until the onions are soft. The sauce can now be rubbed through a sieve. However, it is far better to remove and discard the plum stones (the number were noted) and purée the sauce in batches in a food processor.

Reheat the sauce to blend, and pour into hot, clean bottles and seal. The longer this sauce is kept the better.

Makes about 4 litres.

Prune Sauce

Superb with cheese or cold meats.

500g pitted prunes
150g raisins
500g white sugar
5 cups malt vinegar
½ teaspoon cayenne pepper
⅛ teaspoon ground cloves
¼ teaspoon ground allspice
½ teaspoon salt
2cm piece fresh ginger, sliced

Combine all the ingredients in a large saucepan. Bring to the boil and simmer, partially covered, for several hours until the prunes are very tender. Add more vinegar if necessary.

Strain the sauce through a fine sieve, pushing as much through as possible.

Pour into hot, clean bottles and seal.

Makes about 1 litre.

Quince Sauce

A very tasty, aromatic and spicy sauce that is quite different from the other fruit sauces. As well as the usual uses, try it with fried or grilled fish and with Chinese food too.

2 kg quinces
1 kg apples
500g onions
1 tablespoon cayenne pepper
3 tablespoons salt
1 tablespoon whole cloves
2 tablespoons whole allspice
1 kg sugar
3 litres malt vinegar

Finely chop the quinces and apples, discarding the cores. Finely chop the onions. Combine all the ingredients in a large saucepan and mix well. Slowly bring to the boil, stirring until the sugar is dissolved.

Cook very gently for about 3 hours, until thick and very pulpy. Push as much through a sieve as possible, and pour into hot, clean bottles and seal.

Makes about 5 litres.

Redcurrant Ketchup

Serve cold or hot with poultry, game or fish, or try it with barbecued meat. This is not as thick as the usual fruit sauce.

3 litres redcurrant juice
750 ml white vinegar
1 kg sugar
1 tablespoon ground cinnamon
¼ teaspoon cayenne pepper
1 teaspoon ground cloves
1 teaspoon ground allspice
1 teaspoon salt

Make the redcurrant juice by barely covering the redcurrants with water. Bring to the boil and cook, uncovered, until soft. Rub through a fine sieve to remove the seeds and skins.

Combine the redcurrant juice with the remaining ingredients and boil, uncovered, for 20 minutes.

Pour into hot, clean bottles and seal.

Makes about 3 litres.

Rhubarb Sauce

Although the tangy rhubarb flavour is there, this is a surprisingly smooth sauce. Good with all meats.

1 kg rhubarb
4 cloves garlic
2 teaspoons salt
2 onions
3 cups brown sugar
2½ cups malt vinegar
2 teaspoons grated fresh ginger
½ cinnamon stick
1 teaspoon whole allspice
1 teaspoon ground mace
1 teaspoon black peppercorns

Wash and chop the rhubarb. Crush the garlic in the salt, and chop the onions. In a large saucepan combine the rhubarb, garlic, salt, onions, sugar and vinegar. Tie the spices in muslin and add to the saucepan.

Bring to the boil and cook very slowly, uncovered, for 2 hours, stirring regularly. Remove and discard the spices. Rub the sauce through a sieve, and return the purée to the saucepan. Bring to the boil, then pour into hot, clean bottles and seal.

Makes about 1 litre.

Tamarillo Sauce

Even better than plum sauce. Can be used almost immediately, but matures magnificently with age.

2 kg tamarillos
1 onion
500g apples
500g brown sugar
2 tablespoons salt
2 tablespoons black peppercorns
1 tablespoon whole allspice
1 tablespoon whole cloves
1½ teaspoons cayenne pepper
1 litre vinegar

Peel and chop the tamarillos, onion and apples, and place in a large saucepan with the sugar and salt. Tie the black peppercorns, allspice and cloves in muslin and add to the saucepan along with the cayenne pepper and vinegar.

Bring to the boil and simmer, covered, for about 3 hours, stirring occasionally, until the tamarillos have almost disintegrated. Rub as much of the sauce as possible through a sieve. Pour while still hot into hot, clean bottles and seal.

Makes about 2.5 litres.

Old-Fashioned Tomato Sauce

There has probably been more tomato sauce made through the years than all the other sauces combined. Here is a good example of the old-style tomato sauce; it is sweet and spicy.

2 kg ripe tomatoes
500g apples (golden delicious or other sweet apples)
500g onions
4 tablespoons whole cloves
2 tablespoons whole allspice
1½ tablespoons whole black peppercorns
500g sugar
2 tablespoons salt
¼ teaspoon cayenne pepper
1¼ cups malt vinegar

Coarsely chop the unpeeled tomatoes and apples and coarsely chop the peeled onions. Tie the cloves, allspice and peppercorns in muslin. Combine all the ingredients in a large saucepan. Bring to the boil and cook, uncovered, for 1 hour.

Put the sauce through a mouli or rub as much as possible through a sieve. Mix the sauce well, then pour into warm, clean bottles and seal.

Makes about 2.5 litres.

Bright Red Tomato Sauce

This bright red tomato sauce doesn't use vinegar but uses acid and oils obtained from the chemist. It is a superb sauce, the colour and flavour are not just like the bought one — they are far better.

6 kg ripe tomatoes
5 large onions
50g garlic
50g fresh ginger
6 small dried red chillies
4 tablespoons salt
12 black peppercorns
5 cups sugar

Coarsely chop the unpeeled tomatoes, finely chop the onions, garlic, ginger and chillies. Combine them in a saucepan with salt and peppercorns, bring to the boil, stirring, then gently cook for 2 hours. Put the sauce through a mouli or rub as much as possible through a sieve.

Return the purée to the saucepan and add the sugar. Boil for another 30 minutes.

45 ml glacial acetic acid
10 ml refined or rectified spirit
2 ml oil of cloves
2 ml oil of pimento

These ingredients should be available from the chemist. The refined spirit and the oil of pimento can be omitted if unavailable. Add these ingredients, mix thoroughly, then bottle and seal the sauce.

Makes about 3.5 litres.

Green Tomato Sauce

Don't ask why, but this is also known as *Governor's Sauce*. This sharp and spicy sauce is great with sliced cold beef and tongue. Add a little to mayonnaise for a special salad dressing. Or simply use it instead of red tomato sauce.

1.5 kg green tomatoes, sliced
500g onions, sliced
1 cup salt
2 cups brown sugar
1½ teaspoons white pepper
8 small dried red chillies, crushed
1½ teaspoons dry mustard
1 teaspoon ground cloves
cider vinegar

Make alternate layers of tomatoes, onions and salt in a large bowl, making sure salt is the last layer. Let stand overnight or for 24 hours. Drain the vegetables and rinse them well under cold running water.

Combine all the ingredients in a large saucepan and add enough vinegar to almost cover the mixture. Bring to the boil and cook over moderate heat for about 3 hours, until soft. Stir occasionally to prevent burning.

Allow the mixture to cool for about 1 hour before puréeing in the blender or putting through a food mill to make a thick sauce, or rubbing through a sieve to make a thinner sauce.

Pour into clean bottles or jars and seal.
Makes about 2.5 litres.

Walnut Ketchup

Made from undeveloped green walnuts, this ketchup is thin in consistency and thick in taste like its look-alike, worcestershire sauce. Use in a similar way.

100 immature green walnuts
6 tablespoons salt
8 cloves garlic, crushed
125g shallots or onions, finely chopped
10 cups malt vinegar
2 teaspoons whole cloves
4 tablespoons black peppercorns
2 teaspoons ground mace
50g can anchovies, finely chopped

The walnuts should be so soft that they can be pierced with a needle. Finely chop the walnuts and place them in a large bowl with the salt, garlic, shallots and vinegar. Let stand for 2 weeks. Mash and stir daily.

Strain the liquid and place in a large saucepan with the spices and anchovies. Bring to the boil and cook, uncovered, for about 40 minutes, then strain.

Pour into hot, clean bottles and seal when cold.

Makes about 1.5 litres.

Worcestershire Sauce

The origin of this sauce is Indian. The story is that about 1837 an ex-governor of Bengal went into one of the several shops in Worcester belonging to Mr Lea and Mr Perrins with a recipe for a sauce which he asked them to make up for him. This they did, but the result was not to his satisfaction and he refused to accept it. Several years later Mr Lea and Mr Perrins, when cleaning out the cellar, came upon a barrel containing the rejected sauce and tasted it. It was excellent. As they still had the recipe they made more and began to produce it for local consumption. Soon it was popular and found its way into the kitchen of many noble families. The fame of the sauce spread, mainly by word of mouth and through the pursers of the old passenger steamships. They discovered it was adapted "for every variety of dish — from turtle to beef, from salmon to steaks, to all of which it gives great relish".

Although the original firm still continues to manufacture the sauce, others claim they are using the original recipe.

Here is a recipe that is very close to that of the ex-governor of Bengal, though it probably has far fewer ingredients.

5 cups malt vinegar
1 kg treacle
2 teaspoons salt
3cm piece green ginger, finely chopped
4 cloves garlic, finely chopped
2 tablespoons ground cloves
1 teaspoon cayenne pepper

Combine all the ingredients in a saucepan. Bring to the boil and cook gently, uncovered, for 20 minutes. Cover and let stand overnight.

Next day, strain and bottle. Ready for use immediately, but shake before using.

The Oils

Aromatically infused by fresh herbs, fragrant culinary oils have many uses: they can be used in salad dressings, in meat and poultry marinades, to flavour vegetables, and are invaluable when barbecuing and grilling. They are also great for frying croutons for salads or soups.

The oils look attractive and a row of bottles at a barbecue, for instance, is not only useful for brushing on the barbecuing foods but fun to use — and because they are fun to look at, they make an excellent conversation piece.

Depending on the flavour you want, choose either a strong oil like olive oil, or a neutral-tasting oil like safflower oil.

Fresh herbs have more aroma than their dried counterparts, but be careful when using fresh herbs: they contain moisture which may cause decay after several weeks. After washing the herbs you must *thoroughly* dry them.

Check the oils weekly and strain into another bottle should they start to show signs of decay, that is, to go cloudy. Although cloudy oils tend to look unsightly they should not be harmful unless they start to smell putrid.

Flavour these oils in small batches, one or two cups at a time, since with time, the oil can become rancid. You should taste to test, as the oil on the rims of bottles can be quite strong whereas the oil itself is still sweet. Also, use bottles with small necks to lessen exposure to air and help keep the oil fresh-tasting. Store away from light.

The effects of the flavourings become apparent within a week, but grow on standing to a maximum of several months. If flavours become too intense, simply dilute the oil.

To prepare fresh herbs, rinse them well in cold water, then allow to thoroughly dry on paper towels. Use the hot water cupboard if necessary. It is important that the herbs are completely dry before being used. However, don't dehydrate them by drying for too long.

Green Peppercorn Oil

3 teaspoons drained green peppercorns
¾ cup peanut oil

For maximum effect, thread the green peppercorns on to nylon thread, like a string of beads. Place them in a small bottle and pour the oil over. Leave to mature for at least 3 days, shaking the bottle daily.

Garlic Oil

fresh garlic
olive oil

Peel and thread the garlic cloves on to a small bamboo skewer, long enough to reach the top of the bottle. Place the skewered garlic in the bottle and fill the bottle with olive oil. When you have the garlic flavour you want or the garlic starts to develop a fuzzy haze, remove the garlic.

Dill Oil

2 or 3 large seed heads of fresh dill
olive oil

Push, stem first, the fresh dill into a small bottle of 1 or 2-cup capacity. Fill with olive oil—extra-virgin if desired—close tightly and let stand for at least 7 days before using.

Fragrant Spice Oil

3 or 4 thin slices fresh ginger
small piece cinnamon stick
3 or 4 small dried red chillies
1 teaspoon coriander seed, slightly crushed
1 teaspoon cumin seed, slightly crushed
peanut oil or salad oil

In a small 1 or 2-cup bottle place the ginger, cinnamon stick, chillies, coriander seed and cumin seed. Fill the bottle with peanut oil or salad oil, close tightly and let stand for at least 7 days before using.

Fresh Green Herbs Oil

4 sprigs fresh thyme
4 sprigs fresh tarragon
4 sprigs fresh rosemary
4 sprigs fresh sage
2 fresh bay leaves
1 teaspoon black peppercorns
olive oil

In a 1 or 2-cup bottle stuff the thyme, tarragon, rosemary, sage and bay leaves and add the peppercorns. Fill the bottle with olive oil, close tightly and let stand for 7 days before using.

Herb Oil

fresh herbs
black peppercorns
olive oil

Follow the directions for **Fresh Green Herbs Oil** but loosely
pack the bottle with *one* type of fresh herb, add 1 teaspoon
black peppercorns and top with olive oil. Close tightly and let
stand for 7 days before using.

Fennel Oil

6 slender fresh fennel stems
1 tablespoon fennel seed, slightly crushed
olive oil

In a 1 or 2-cup bottle stuff the fennel stems and add the fennel
seed. Fill the bottle with olive oil—extra-virgin if desired—
and let stand for at least 7 days before using.

The Pickles

Pickles consist of vegetables, and fruits, often soaked in brine or salt, and stored in vinegar that has been boiled with spices. Salt and sugar are frequently added also, in quantities varied to individual taste.

This chapter embraces three types of pickles: pickled vegetables, such as onions and okra; pickled or spiced fruits, such as plums and loquats; and mustard pickles, such as Chow Chow and pickled cabbage.

In all cases the vegetables or fruits in the pickles remain identifiable — some whole, others in pieces — whereas in chutneys they generally become immersed in the overall flavour.

Pickles, therefore, are still crunchy, and this is achieved by either soaking the vegetables in brine to remove some of the moisture, or especially in the case of fruit, by simply not cooking them for too long. Boiling in an alum solution gives crispness to some fruits and vegetables. Alum is available from the chemist.

Pickles are a way of preserving fruits and vegetables, but the need for a relish to accompany bland foods is still the basic reason for pickling, rather than storing the produce for a later date.

Remember there are more pickles to follow in the chapter 'The Refrigerator Pickles': these are more instant pickles and are not long keepers.

Pickled or spiced fruits are quite ubiquitous: as well as going with savoury foods both as relishes and edible garnishes, they are often served with ice-cream, or by themselves, or with cheese as a refreshing dessert.

When packing the vegetables or fruit into the jars, bear in mind the presentation. A jar of pickles can be extremely attractive when arranged with care.

If there is not enough liquid to cover the fruit or vegetables in the jars completely, simply boil up some more vinegar and top up the jars. And make sure you get out as many air bubbles as possible before covering or sealing the jars.

Several different pickled vegetables or fruits make great toothpick food to serve with drinks or simply as nibbles. And pickled vegetables can often be served as special salads or as an ingredient in salads. Pickles are usually ready to eat in about three or four weeks and can be stored for about six months to a year.

Pickled Apples

Delicious with pork and ham, or cheese or salad.

3.5 kg apples
6 cups brown sugar
4 cups cider vinegar
1 cup water
2 x 5cm pieces stick cinnamon
1½ teaspoons cloves

Wash the unpeeled apples, then cut into quarters or eighths and core them. Combine the sugar, vinegar, water and spices and boil for 10 minutes. Drop the apples into the syrup and boil for several minutes, until the apples are lightly cooked. Carefully pack the apples into hot, clean jars, cover with the hot syrup and seal. If there is not enough syrup, top the jars with hot vinegar.
Makes about 7 litres.

Spiced Apricots

Delicious with ham, pork and other hot or cold meats. Peaches and nectarines can also be spiced this way but should be scalded and skinned before halving and removing the stones.

1.5 kg apricots
2 cups white vinegar
18 whole cloves
6 whole allspice
1 stick cinnamon
1 kg white sugar

Split the apricots in half and discard the stones.
   Place the vinegar in a saucepan and bring to the boil. Tie the spices in muslin and add to the vinegar. Add the sugar and dissolve slowly. Once sugar has dissolved, bring vinegar to the boil again and add the apricots, rounded side down. Poach the apricots very gently for about 10 minutes, until barely

tender. Don't overcook as the halves must remain intact.

Lift out the fruit with a slotted spoon and pack into hot, clean jars. Boil the liquid hard for about 3 minutes to reduce it a little, then pour it over the apricots and seal at once. *Makes about 1.5 litres.*

Artichoke Pickle

This marvellous mustard-artichoke pickle is especially good with roast beef but try it with other meats and cheeses.

750g Jerusalem artichokes
3 red or green peppers
3 medium onions
½ cup salt
5½ cups white vinegar
2 cups water
250g sugar
2 tablespoons dry mustard
1 tablespoon turmeric
2 teaspoons celery seed
1 teaspoon mustard seed

Scrub and wash the artichokes well. Core and seed the peppers and peel the onions. Finely chop the artichokes, peppers and onions. Mix them together in a large bowl, sprinkle the salt over and let stand for 12 hours.

Squeeze out as much liquid as possible. Combine 2 cups vinegar with the 2 cups cold water and pour over the vegetables. Let stand for 24 hours.

Drain well and discard the liquid. In a saucepan combine the remaining 3½ cups vinegar with the sugar, then heat and stir only until the sugar is just dissolved. Remove from heat and allow to cool. Stir in the mustard, turmeric, celery seed and mustard seed. Pour this over the vegetables and if the mixture is not moist enough add extra vinegar.

Pour into clean jars and seal.
Makes about 2 litres.

Pickled Artichoke Hearts

These are not difficult to do and are not really any more time consuming than other pickles. Make sure the artichokes are early season ones, small and plump, before the choke has had time to commence growing. If it has, scoop it out with a spoon.

For each 600 ml Agee jar:

about 8 fresh young artichokes
lemon juice
salt
½ teaspoon pickling spice
1 clove garlic, peeled
2 bay leaves
1 slice lemon
olive oil
dry white wine

Prepare the artichokes: with a sharp knife cut off the coarse outer leaves and remove about two-thirds of the top of the artichoke. Remove the hairy choke if necessary and trim around the outside so that the bottom and only the tender inside leaves are left. Immediately plunge into cold water to which has been added the juice of a lemon or some white vinegar. They will probably darken slightly while you are preparing the rest. However, when the artichoke hearts are brought to the boil they will whiten again. Each 600 ml jar should hold about 8 artichoke hearts.

Bring the artichoke hearts to the boil in water to cover, with the juice of a lemon and a little salt. Simmer until barely tender, then drain and allow to cool enough to handle.

Into the clean jar place the pickling spice and garlic, then pack in the barely cooked artichoke hearts. Push the bay leaves and lemon slice down the sides of the jar. Fill the jar two-thirds full with olive oil, then add the dry white wine — any dry white will suffice — to 1cm from the top. Screw down the Agee seal.

Place a rack or folded cloth in the bottom of a deep saucepan and place the jar of artichokes in the saucepan. Cover the jar with cold water. Bring the water slowly to the boil and boil gently for 30 minutes.

Lift out the jar onto a board and allow to stand for 12 hours before removing the ring band.

Can be eaten in 1 month and should be used within a year before the artichokes get oil-logged. Note that the strained juices make an excellent salad dressing.

Pickled Asparagus

This tastes as good as it looks and makes an excellent finger food with drinks or as a special salad or even an entrée.

2 small onions
750g very thin asparagus
2 red peppers
2 teaspoons salt
5 cups cider vinegar
3 tablespoons sugar
3 tablespoons whole pickling spice
2 cups water

Finely slice the onions. Trim and wash the asparagus and cut the red peppers into thin strips, discarding the seeds. Bring some water to the boil in a saucepan, add the onions, bring back to the boil and simmer for 3 minutes. Remove the onions with a slotted spoon and arrange them on the bottom of two warmed 1-litre jars.

Place the asparagus and red peppers in the saucepan and simmer for 3 minutes. Drain well, then pack the asparagus, cut end down, with the red pepper strips to give a striped effect, in the jars.

Boil the remaining ingredients, uncovered, for 10 minutes, then fill the warmed jars with the strained liquid, and seal by the overflow method. Ready for use in about 2 weeks.

Makes about 2 litres.

Dill Pickled Beans

Hot, crisp and quite delicious. Serve these beans with drinks or use them as a delicious vegetable course, hot or cold, or add a novel touch to salads.

1 kg fresh young green beans
4 cloves garlic
4 sprigs fresh dill
1 teaspoon cayenne pepper
2 tablespoons salt
4 cups white vinegar
4 cups water

Wash and rinse two 5-cup jars. Trim the beans, leaving them whole, and pack them into the hot jars. Into each jar place 2 cloves garlic, 2 sprigs fresh dill and ½ teaspoon cayenne pepper.
  Heat the salt, vinegar and water to boiling in a saucepan and pour over the beans in the jars. Seal the jars. Keep for 2 weeks or longer before using.

Herbed Pickled Beans

Serve these scrumptious green beans with cold meats, as a salad or as part of a mixed hors d'oeuvres platter. They go particularly well with beer too.

500g young French beans
2½ cups white vinegar
1 small onion, thinly sliced
1 tablespoon sugar
2 tablespoons whole black peppercorns
2 bay leaves
¼ teaspoon mace
1 large sprig fresh thyme or tarragon
5 cups water
1 tablespoon salt

Top and tail the beans, leaving them whole.

In a large saucepan combine the vinegar, onion, sugar, peppercorns, bay leaves, mace and thyme. Bring to the boil, cover the saucepan and boil for 1 minute. Remove from heat and allow to cool.

In another saucepan bring the 5 cups water and the salt to the boil, add the prepared beans and simmer for 2–3 minutes, until the beans are bright green. Drain and rinse under cold running water to cool the beans quickly. Pat dry with paper towels.

Pack the beans upright into a clean, 1-litre jar. Strain the vinegar mixture into the jar to cover the beans. Add more vinegar if necessary.

Seal and store in a cool place for about 2 months before using.

Makes 1 litre.

Pickled Beetroot

A very simple yet effective way to preserve beetroot.

beetroot
2 cups sugar
4 cups malt vinegar
3 cups strained cooking water

Scrub the beetroot very gently to remove all dirt. Cook in boiling water to cover for about 1 hour, until tender. Allow to cool, then peel and slice, reserving the cooking water.

In another saucepan combine the sugar, malt vinegar and cooking water, and bring to the boil. Add the sliced beetroot and bring back to the boil.

Pack the beetroot into hot, clean jars, cover with the hot liquid and seal.

Beetroot and Orange Pickle

Serve this as a side dish with simple grilled meats or barbecues.
The pickle is ready to eat as soon as it is made.

1 kg raw beetroot
1 medium cooking apple
500g onions
thinly peeled rind of 1 small orange
2 tablespoons finely chopped fresh ginger
2 cloves garlic, crushed
1¼ cups wine vinegar
250g brown sugar

Peel the beetroot and cut it into large cubes. Peel, core and
slice the apple, and finely chop the onions. Finely chop the
orange rind and mix it with all the prepared ingredients in a
large saucepan. Add the ginger, garlic, vinegar and sugar.

Bring the pickle to the boil, cover the saucepan and reduce
the heat. Simmer gently for about 1½ hours, stirring occasionally. The beetroot should be in chunks and the pickle quite
juicy. Remove the lid and cook for a further 20–30 minutes
until the juices thicken.

Transfer the pickle to hot, clean jars and seal.
Makes about 1.5 litres.

Gingered Beetroot

A sweet pickle, excellent with cold lamb and other meats.

5 cups peeled and thinly sliced raw beetroot
500g sugar
25g preserved or crystallised ginger, chopped
juice of 1 lemon
1 cup malt vinegar

In a basin combine the beetroot, sugar and ginger and let stand
overnight. Next day, bring all the ingredients to the boil in
a saucepan, and cook gently, uncovered, for about 1 hour,

until the pickle is thickened and clear.
Transfer to small, hot, clean jars and seal.
Makes about 1 litre.

Blackberry Pickle

Use with all kinds of meats and poultry or with cheese.
Boysenberries could be substituted for the blackberries.

1 kg ripe blackberries
4 cups sugar
2 tablespoons ground allspice
2 tablespoons ground ginger
2 cups white vinegar

Place the blackberries in a saucepan with the sugar and spices.
Carefully mix them and let stand for 12 hours or overnight.
   Heat the vinegar to boiling, then pour over the berries. Bring
slowly to the boil and cook very gently for 30 minutes, stirring
occasionally, and carefully to avoid breaking the berries.
   Remove from heat and allow to cool. Spoon into clean jars
and seal.
Makes about 2 litres.

Brinjal Pickle

Brinjal means eggplant in Indian and this hot pickle is naturally excellent with curries — or cold meats too.

1 kg eggplant
2 tablespoons salt
5 large onions, sliced
2 cups oil
1 teaspoon ground coriander
1 teaspoon cumin
3 tablespoons turmeric
100g root ginger, grated
100g green chillies, finely chopped
75g garlic, crushed
100g sultanas
750 ml malt vinegar

Cut the eggplant into small cubes, leaving the skin on. Sprinkle with the salt and let stand for at least 6 hours, then drain well.

Gently fry the onions in the oil, without browning, until limp. Add the spices, ginger, chillies and garlic and gently fry, stirring, for a few minutes. Add the sultanas, vinegar and eggplant and continue cooking until the eggplant is tender.

Spoon into hot, clean jars and seal.

Makes about 3 litres.

Pickled Broccoli with Tarragon

Crisp and green and absolutely marvellous as an hors d'oeuvre or as a special salad.

1.5 kg broccoli
½ cup salt
2 litres water
3 tablespoons whole pickling spice
1 tablespoon black peppercorns
3 cups white vinegar
1 cup water
¼ cup salt
1 bunch (about 50g) fresh tarragon

Cut the broccoli into flowerets and peel and slice the stalk. Place it in a bowl, sprinkle with the ½ cup salt and pour over the 2 litres water. Let stand overnight.

Next day, bring the broccoli to the boil in the brine, then rinse the broccoli thoroughly in cold water. Pack it into hot, clean jars.

Tie the pickling spice and peppercorns in muslin. Combine them with the remaining ingredients in a saucepan, bring to the boil and boil for 10 minutes. Pour the hot vinegar mixture over the broccoli, filling the jars and making sure that the tarragon is distributed evenly among the jars, then seal.

Makes about 2 litres.

Pickled Brussels Sprouts

You can very successfully pickle cabbage so why not brussels sprouts. These are great with drinks or added to a green salad.

2.75 kg brussels sprouts, trimmed and halved
salt
2 litres white vinegar
1 cup brown sugar
½ cup mustard seed
2 tablespoons whole cloves
2 nutmegs, broken in pieces
2 tablespoons whole allspice
3 tablespoons black peppercorns
2 tablespoons celery seed
5 bay leaves, broken in pieces

Prepare the brussels sprouts. Sprinkle them with salt and let stand overnight. Next day, rinse them well in cold water.

In a saucepan combine the white vinegar, brown sugar and mustard seed. Tie the remaining spices in muslin and add to the saucepan. Bring to the boil and simmer for 10 minutes. Add the brussels sprouts and bring back to the boil and boil for 1 minute. Remove the spice bag.

Pack the sprouts into hot, clean jars, then pour the liquid over the sprouts and seal the jars. If necessary, fill the jars with extra boiling vinegar.

Makes about 3 litres.

Pickled Cabbage

Serve with cold meats or serve as a salad.

1 medium white cabbage
2 tablespoons salt

Remove the outside or old leaves from the cabbage. Cut it into four and cut out the stalk. Finely slice the cabbage. Place in a large bowl. Sprinkle with the salt and barely cover with cold water. Let stand overnight, then drain well.

Pack tightly into jars, cover with the cold *Spiced Vinegar* and seal. If there is insufficient spiced vinegar, top up the jars with cold vinegar. Let stand for 4 weeks before using.

Spiced Vinegar
5 cups white vinegar
1 tablespoon whole black peppercorns
6 thin slices fresh ginger
½ teaspoon whole allspice
2 tablespoons sugar
1 large onion, finely chopped
1 clove garlic, crushed
3 bay leaves

Combine all the ingredients in a saucepan. Bring to the boil, then allow to cool and strain.

Mustard Cabbage Pickles

Ideal with cheese.

1 large white cabbage
4 medium onions
salt
5 cups vinegar
½ cup flour
1 cup sugar
1 teaspoon curry powder
2 tablespoons dry mustard

Cut the cabbage in quarters, remove the core and slice it finely. Finely chop the onions. Combine the cabbage and onions in a large bowl and sprinkle with salt. Let stand for 24 hours.

Lightly rinse the vegetables with cold water and drain them well. Put the vegetables in a saucepan with 3 cups vinegar, bring to the boil and boil for 20 minutes. Combine the flour, sugar, curry powder and mustard with the remaining 2 cups vinegar, stir into the cabbage and boil for a further 5 minutes. If the mixture is too thick add a little more vinegar.

Pour into hot, clean jars and seal.
Makes about 3 litres.

Pickled Red Cabbage

Pickled red cabbage has many traditional uses but is great as a salad with steamed fish or a light paté or terrine.

1 red cabbage
2 tablespoons salt
5 cups white vinegar
25g whole pickling spice

Remove the outside or old leaves from the cabbage, cut into four, cut out the stalks, then slice across very thinly. Place in a bowl, sprinkle with the salt, put a small plate on top of the cabbage and place a weight on the plate. Let stand for 24 hours.

Combine the vinegar and pickling spice in a saucepan. Bring to the boil and boil for a few minutes, then cool and strain.

Pack the cabbage lightly into jars. Pour the strained, spiced vinegar over the cabbage, making sure it is covered, then seal the jars tightly. Ready for use in about 6 days.

Makes about 2 litres.

Spiced Cantaloupe

The cantaloupes must be ripe but still firm. Any other similar type of aromatic musk melon could be used. Serve with cold cuts, or spear on toothpicks and serve as an unusual cocktail party food.

3 ripe, firm cantaloupes (about 500g each)
1½ teaspoons alum
8 cups water
3 cups sugar
2 cups white vinegar
2 pieces stick cinnamon
1 tablespoon allspice
1½ teaspoons whole cloves

Cut the cantaloupes in half, scoop out the seeds and make the flesh into balls with a melon-baller. Dissolve the alum in the water in a large saucepan. Bring to the boil, add the cantaloupe and cook gently for 15 minutes. Drain the cantaloupe and wash well under cold water.

In the same saucepan combine the sugar, vinegar and the spices tied in muslin. Bring to the boil, add the melon and cook slowly for about 45 minutes, until the fruit is transparent.

Discard the spice bag and spoon the melon into hot, clean jars. Cover with the syrup and seal.
Makes about 1.5 litres.

Cauliflower Pickle

An excellent yellow, mustard pickle.

1 large cauliflower
4 large onions
2 tablespoons salt
7 cups malt vinegar
2 cups golden syrup
2 tablespoons mustard
½ cup flour
1½ teaspoons curry powder
1½ teaspoons turmeric

Cut the cauliflower and onions finely. Sprinkle with the salt and leave overnight. Cover with cold water — to wash off some of the salt — and drain well.

In a saucepan boil the cauliflower and onions in 5 cups vinegar for 20 minutes. Mix the remaining ingredients with the remaining 2 cups vinegar. Stir into the boiling mixture. Bring back to the boil and boil gently, stirring, for 5 minutes.

Pour into hot, clean jars and seal.
Makes about 4 litres.

Cauliflower and Pineapple Pickle

Cauliflower and pineapple are an excellent combination, especially in the mustard pickle.

750g onions, finely sliced
1 medium cauliflower, cut into small flowerets
1½ tablespoons salt
white vinegar
400g can crushed pineapple
¼ cup flour
2 teaspoons dry mustard
1 tablespoon curry powder
2 tablespoons sugar

Combine the onions and cauliflower in a large bowl. Sprinkle with the salt and let stand overnight.

Next day, drain the vegetables and put them in a large saucepan. Barely cover with white vinegar, bring to the boil, and simmer, covered, for 15 minutes.

Add the pineapple, and the flour, mustard, curry powder and sugar, mixed to a smooth paste with some cold vinegar. Stir until thickened, then cook gently, uncovered, for a further 10 minutes.

Spoon into hot, clean jars and seal.
Makes about 3 litres.

Minted Cauliflower Pickle

The combination of cool fresh mint and hot cayenne makes a very interesting cauliflower pickle.

1.5 kg cauliflower
1.5 kg onions
4 tablespoons salt
7 cups cold water
1 cup sugar
4 tablespoons very finely chopped mint
6 cups white vinegar
1 tablespoon turmeric
¾ cup flour
1 teaspoon ground allspice
1 teaspoon cayenne pepper
1 teaspoon curry powder

Cut the cauliflower into small flowerets. Halve the onions and finely slice them. Combine the vegetables in a bowl, sprinkle with the salt, pour over the cold water, and let stand overnight. Drain well but do not rinse.

Place the vegetables in a saucepan, add the sugar, mint and vinegar. Mix the remaining ingredients together with enough water to form a smooth paste. Stir into the vegetables. Slowly bring to the boil, stirring, and cook gently for 10 minutes, stirring constantly.

Pour into hot, clean jars and seal.
Makes about 4.5 litres.

Chow Chow

A slightly sweet, thick mustard pickle, the American version of **Piccalilli**. Almost any white or green vegetable could be used but it seems mandatory to include cauliflower, beans and cucumber as well as the onions.

2 kg prepared mixed vegetables: cauliflower cut into flowerets, sliced green beans, peeled, seeded and chopped cucumber, broccoli in small flowerets, sliced celery or green tomatoes cut in wedges
250g onions, halved and sliced
¼ cup salt
2 litres water
1 cup sugar
½ cup flour
2 teaspoons turmeric
2 tablespoons mustard
1 teaspoon celery seeds
4½ cups white vinegar

Place the prepared vegetables in a large saucepan and cover with the salt and water. Cover and let stand overnight.

Next day, heat slowly to boiling point and simmer for 5 minutes. Drain well.

In another saucepan combine the sugar, flour, turmeric, mustard and celery seeds. Mix to a paste with some of the vinegar, then add the remainder of the vinegar. Slowly bring to the boil, stirring constantly, then simmer for a few minutes. Add to the vegetables.

Pour into hot, clean jars and seal.

Makes about 4 litres.

Green Tomato Chow Chow

A dark, thick and strong sweet-sharp pickle.

3 kg green tomatoes
5 large onions

500g treacle
2 tablespoons curry powder
2 tablespoons dry mustard
1 tablespoon salt
2 litres malt vinegar
5 tablespoons flour

Slice the green tomatoes and halve and slice the onions. Combine the vegetables with the treacle, curry powder, mustard, salt and vinegar in a large saucepan. Bring to the boil and boil very gently for 1 hour. Mix the flour to a smooth paste with extra vinegar, stir into the chow chow and slowly cook for a further 20 minutes, stirring occasionally.

Pour into hot, clean jars and seal.
Makes about 6 litres.

Spiced Cherries

Leave the stalks on and these make a very attractive garnish for meat, poultry or game dishes. There is no need to remove the stones either. If the stalks are on the cherries, people expect the stones to still be there too.

1 kg cherries
6 cups white vinegar
750g sugar
12 cloves
1 tablespoon peppercorns
2 cinnamon sticks

Pick over the fruit and remove and discard any that is speckled. Put the rest in a large warmed jar.

In a saucepan combine the vinegar, sugar, cloves, peppercorns and cinnamon sticks. Bring to the boil and boil for 2 minutes, then pour the hot vinegar over the cherries. Make sure the fruit is completely covered. Let stand for 1 week, loosely covered.

Pour off the vinegar into a saucepan and bring it to the boil, then pour over the fruit. As soon as it is cold, seal the jar.
Makes about 2 litres.

Choko Pickles

A sharp mustard pickle in which the chokos retain their delicious crispish texture.

1.5 kg chokos
1.5 kg onions
1 cup salt
4 litres cold water
1 cup sugar
1 cup flour
2 tablespoons mustard
1 tablespoon turmeric
1 teaspoon curry powder
1 teaspoon cayenne pepper
2.5 litres malt vinegar

Peel, quarter and core the chokos. Peel and halve the onions. Slice them both finely, and soak overnight in a brine made of the salt and cold water.

Next day, bring the vegetables to the boil in the brine, then strain off the brine, draining the vegetables well.

Mix the dry ingredients together in a saucepan with enough of the vinegar to make a smooth paste. Gradually add all the vinegar, then slowly bring to the boil, stirring constantly, until it is thick and bubbling. Add the vegetables, bring back to the boil, and cook, very slowly, for 10 minutes.

Pour into hot, clean jars and seal.

Makes about 6 litres.

Spiced Chokos

Be careful to undercook rather than overcook the chokos so that the result is like crisp pears. The texture and spiciness go well with cold lamb and beef.

6 medium chokos
3½ cups white vinegar
2 tablespoons sugar
1 teaspoon salt
pinch mace
6 peppercorns
2 bay leaves
½ teaspoon cloves
3 chillies, split

Peel the chokos and cut them into quarters lengthwise. Remove the cores, put in boiling salted water and simmer for 5–10 minutes or until almost crisp-tender. Drain well, then pack the chokos into hot, clean jars.

Heat the vinegar, sugar, salt, mace, peppercorns, bay leaves and cloves and boil for 3 minutes.

Pour the strained liquid over the chokos, adding a piece of chilli pepper to each jar, and seal.

Makes about 2 litres.

Pickled Clementine Mandarins

Serve with pork, ham, poultry or duck, either hot or cold.

1 kg clementine mandarins
700g sugar
2½ cups water
1 cup white vinegar
1 stick cinnamon, broken
1½ teaspoons whole cloves
1½ teaspoons whole allspice

Wash the clementines. Make a skin-deep cut around the centre of each fruit. Drop the fruit into an abundance of boiling water, cook for 2 minutes, then drain.

Dissolve the sugar in the water, add the fruit and cook quickly until the fruit begins to look transparent. Do not overcook, about 15 minutes should be enough. Cover and allow to stand overnight.

Next day, lift the fruit out of the syrup. To the syrup add the vinegar, cinnamon, cloves and allspice, and boil for 2 minutes. Pour this spiced syrup over the clementines. Cover and leave until next day. Repeat this draining and boiling the syrup (for 2 minutes) for 4 days.

On the last day, pack the fruit into clean jars, pour the heated syrup over and seal.

Coconut Pickle

An excellent, well-flavoured crunchy pickle. It is great with curries, spicy meat dishes, fish dishes or sprinkled on a salad.

1 coconut
250g onions
3 cloves garlic, crushed
1 stick cinnamon
1 teaspoon salt
½ teaspoon ground ginger
⅛ teaspoon chilli powder

1 ¼ cups cider vinegar
100g sugar

Pierce the coconut and drain the liquid into a large saucepan.
Break open the coconut and remove all the coconut flesh, with
the inner brown skin, from the hard shell. Grate the flesh on
a coarse grater and add to the saucepan.

Finely chop the onions and add them to the saucepan along
with the remaining ingredients. Bring the mixture to the boil,
stirring continuously, to combine all the ingredients. Cover
the saucepan, reduce the heat and allow the pickle to simmer
for 30 minutes, stirring occasionally, until the juices are
thickened.

Spoon into hot, clean jars and seal.
Makes about 1.5 litres.

Courgette Pickle

A good sort of variation on bread and butter pickles.

1 kg courgettes
2 medium onions
½ cup salt
2½ cups white vinegar
½ cup white sugar
1 teaspoon celery seed
1 teaspoon mustard seed
1 teaspoon turmeric
½ teaspoon dry mustard

Wash, trim and finely slice the courgettes. Finely slice the
onions. Put the vegetables in a bowl and cover with water.
Sprinkle with the salt and let stand for 1 hour. Drain but do
not rinse.

Mix the remaining ingredients and bring to the boil, then
pour over the vegetables and let stand for 1 hour.

Bring everything to the boil and simmer gently, covered, for
10 minutes. Stir occasionally, gently to prevent breaking the
courgettes. Spoon into hot, clean jars and seal.
Makes about 1.5 litres.

Pickled Yellow Courgettes

Other spices of choice may be added to the basic pickling solution, and green courgettes, scallopini or other small summer squash could be substituted for the yellow courgettes.

8 cups sliced yellow courgettes (about 1 kg)
2 cups sliced onions
1 cup diced green pepper
1 tablespoon salt
2 cups cider vinegar
3½ cups sugar
1 teaspoon celery seed
1 teaspoon mustard seed

Combine the courgettes, onions and green pepper. Sprinkle with the salt and let stand for 1 hour. Drain well but do not rinse. Combine the vegetables with the vinegar, sugar and seeds. Boil gently for 10 minutes.

Carefully pack the courgette mixture into hot, clean jars, then cover with the hot syrup and seal.

Makes about 1.5 litres.

Pickled Crab Apples

Serve with hot or cold meats, especially lamb, hogget, ham or duck.

2 kg ripe crab apples
3 cups cider vinegar
4 cups brown sugar
1 teaspoon whole cloves
5cm stick cinnamon
3 strips lemon peel

Leave the stalks on the crab apples. Prick each apple with a fork to prevent bursting when cooking. Combine the crab apples with the remaining ingredients in a large saucepan and gently simmer for about 20 minutes or until the crab apples are just tender and still whole.

Pack the crab apples into hot, clean jars, then pour the syrup over, and seal by the overflow method. Let stand for 1 month before using.

Makes about 3 litres.

Bread and Butter Pickles

Probably the best cucumber pickles you've ever tasted. These are superb on buttered brown bread — hence the name. They also go marvellously well with cold meats and cheeses.

8 large cucumbers, unpeeled
3 large onions
4 large green peppers
1 cup salt
9 cups cold water
1.8 litres malt vinegar
1.5 kg white sugar
1 tablespoon turmeric
1 teaspoon mustard seed
1 teaspoon celery seed

Wash and slice the cucumbers, slice the onions and green peppers. Combine the vegetables in a large bowl, sprinkle with the salt and add the cold water. Let stand for 3 hours, then drain thoroughly without rinsing.

In a large saucepan combine the remaining ingredients. Heat to boiling, then add the vegetables. Bring to boiling point again but do not boil.

Pack into hot, clean jars and seal. Chill before serving.

Makes about 6 litres.

To make *Curried Bread and Butter Pickles* omit the turmeric and add 2 teaspoons curry powder.

Dill Pickles

What can one say about dill pickles? There are hundreds of ways of making them but, basically, dill pickles are cucumbers with dill leaves or seed heads, all matured in a brine or vinegar solution for several weeks. A true dill cucumber is in-between the size of a gherkin and a small cucumber. However, gherkins or slightly immature cucumbers — before the seeds fully develop — can be used for dill pickles. Dill pickles are ideal with just about any savoury food. This recipe is probably the best you'll find anywhere.

1–1.25 kg medium-sized gherkins (about 10cm) or same-size immature cucumbers or young cucumbers cut about the same size
3 1/2 cups white vinegar or cider vinegar
1 1/2 cups water
2 tablespoons salt
1 1/2 teaspoons alum
1/2 cup white sugar
4 large heads fresh dill
1 teaspoon mustard seed

Wash the gherkins. Combine the vinegar, water, salt, alum and sugar in a bowl. Add the gherkins and let stand overnight.

Next day, drain the liquid into a large saucepan, and bring it to the boil. Have the hot, clean jars and lids ready.

Add the gherkins to the boiling liquid and simmer for 8–10 minutes but do not allow to boil. Pack the gherkins into the jars, placing a head of dill in the bottom, sprinkle with mustard seeds and finish with a sprig of dill on top. Pack both jars and keep them warm by standing in hot water.

Bring the vinegar mixture back to the boil and pour over the gherkins. Release any air bubbles, and seal by the overflow method. Ready for use in several weeks.

Makes two 5-cup jars.

Canadian Dill Pickles

This is a comparatively easy way of making dill pickles, by quantity rather than by weight.

gherkins or small cucumbers
fresh dill
black peppercorns
garlic
whole cloves
salt
sugar
white vinegar
boiling water

Wash enough gherkins — or cucumbers to slice or cut into chunks — to fill a 1-litre jar.

Before putting the gherkins in the jar, place a sprig of fresh dill, 5 ground black peppercorns, 1 peeled whole clove garlic and 1 whole clove, then pack the gherkins in the jar. Add 1 teaspoon salt and 3 tablespoons sugar.

Stand the jar in hot water to expand the glass, then slowly add 1 cup boiling white vinegar and top the jar with boiling water. Seal by the overflow method.

The pickles are ready for use in 1 month.

Pickled Gherkins

These gherkins are perfect — crisp-tender and succulent.

50 gherkins
brine
1 tablespoon salt
1 teaspoon whole allspice
2 tablespoons mustard seed
1.5 litres white vinegar
1½ cups sugar
pinch cloves and mace
1 teaspoon white peppercorns

Wash the gherkins and rub off black horny surface. Make a brine (100g salt to 600 ml water) to cover the gherkins. Leave to soak in the cold brine for 24 hours.

Make up a pickling solution by boiling the remaining ingredients together for 10 minutes. Drain the gherkins, rinse them well under cold water, then dry them well.

Add the gherkins to the pickling solution and boil for 2 minutes. Strain the vinegar into the large container, reserving the spices, then add the gherkins. Make sure the gherkins are covered by the solution.

Next day, pour off the vinegar and boil with the spices again. Pack the gherkins into hot, clean jars and pour the boiling hot vinegar and spices over the gherkins. Seal by the overflow method. Store for several weeks before using.

Cucumber Pickle

Cucumber and mustard make a very good mustard pickle that goes especially well with cheese or corned beef.

2 kg cucumbers
2 kg onions
1 cup salt
3 litres malt vinegar

1 cup flour
1 cup sugar
6 tablespoons dry mustard
1 tablespoon turmeric

Peel and finely slice the cucumbers and onions. Combine them in a large bowl and sprinkle with the salt. Allow to stand for 24 hours, mixing the vegetables occasionally.

Drain the vegetables and squeeze out as much liquid as possible. In a large saucepan, bring the vinegar to the boil and add the drained vegetables. Bring back to the boil and cook gently until the vegetables are just tender.

In a bowl combine the flour, sugar, mustard and turmeric, and mix to a smooth paste with some cold vinegar. Stir into the boiling vegetables, and cook for several minutes, stirring often.

Spoon into hot, clean jars and seal.
Makes about 7 litres.

Pickled Eggs

Serve as a snack, or an hors d'oeuvres platter or with winter salads or cold meats.

12 hard-boiled eggs, shelled and cooled
2½ cups white wine vinegar
1 tablespoon pickling spice
small piece of orange rind, about 5cm long
3 cloves garlic, peeled

Prepare the eggs. Place the vinegar, pickling spice, orange rind and garlic in a saucepan. Bring to the boil, cover and simmer for 10 minutes. Remove from heat and leave until mixture is completely cold.

Meanwhile, put 6 eggs in each of two clean half-litre jars with wide necks and screw-top lids. When the vinegar is cold, strain it over the eggs, making sure they are completely covered with liquid. Screw the lids on tightly and store for about 6 weeks to allow the flavour of the pickled eggs to develop.

Mustard Pickled Eggs

Great with a ploughman's lunch, or as an anytime snack, or with cold meats.

12 small hard-boiled eggs, shelled
2½ cups spiced vinegar
2 teaspoons mustard
2 teaspoons cornflour
1 teaspoon sugar
½ teaspoon turmeric
1 teaspoon salt

Pack the eggs into clean jars.
   In a saucepan bring the vinegar to the boil. Mix the other ingredients together and mix to a smooth paste with a little cold vinegar. Stir into the boiling vinegar and simmer for 5 minutes. Remove from heat and allow to cool.
   Pour the cold vinegar mixture over the eggs and seal the jars. Let stand for several weeks before using.
Makes 1 litre.

Spiced Eggs

These eggs have a mild curry flavour and are delicious when combined with a little mayonnaise. They make a great standby for an instant entrée and are good with most cold meat dishes.

2½ cups white vinegar
1 small dried red chilli, chopped
6 whole cardamom pods
2 tablespoons coriander seeds
5 whole cloves
½ teaspoon turmeric
4 cloves garlic, crushed
½ teaspoon salt
1 small onion
12 small eggs, hard-boiled and shelled

138

In a saucepan combine the vinegar, chilli, the spices, garlic and salt. Bring to the boil, cover and simmer for 5 minutes. Allow to cool, then strain the vinegar.

Slice the onion into thin rings. Place the onion rings and prepared eggs in a clean 1-litre jar. Pour in the cold vinegar, making sure that it runs between the eggs and covers them completely. Cover and allow to stand for at least 1 week.
Makes 1 litre.

Spiced Feijoas

Aromatic and tangy and superb with pork or ham or any other meat.

2 cups white sugar
2 cups cider vinegar
2 teaspoons cloves
2cm piece root ginger, finely sliced
5cm stick cinnamon
1.5 kg small feijoas

In a saucepan make the spiced syrup by combining the sugar, vinegar, cloves, ginger and cinnamon. Bring to the boil, stirring, until the sugar is dissolved, then simmer for 10 minutes.

Peel the feijoas, and drop them into the syrup. Bring to the boil and simmer for a few minutes until the feijoas are tender.

Carefully pack the feijoas into hot, clean jars and cover them with the hot syrup and seal the jars. If there isn't enough syrup add some hot vinegar to the jars.
Makes about 2.5 litres.

Pickled Figs

Wonderful with hot or cold poultry or game and with ham, and equally good served as a dessert with ice-cream.

1 kg fresh slightly under-ripe figs
1½ cups water
1½ cups malt vinegar
1 cup brown sugar
50g crystallised or preserved ginger, chopped
1 teaspoon whole cloves

Wipe the figs and trim the stems.

Combine the water, vinegar, sugar, ginger and cloves in a saucepan. Bring to the boil, stirring to dissolve the sugar, then simmer, uncovered, for 30 minutes.

Add the figs and cook slowly for about 2 hours, partially covered. Watch carefully towards the end of cooking time to check that the figs do not burn. If necessary, add a little more water.

Pack the figs into hot, clean jars and seal.
Makes about 1.5 litres.

Pickled Garlic

Leave 6 weeks before use . . . if you can! Absolutely more-ish served with cold meats or with the hors d'oeuvres platter.

250g garlic
1 cup white vinegar
¼ teaspoon mustard seed
¼ teaspoon celery seed
3 tablespoons sugar

Peel the garlic and cut the large cloves in half.

Combine the vinegar, mustard seed, celery seed and sugar in a small saucepan, bring to the boil and boil for 5 minutes. Add the prepared garlic, bring to the boil again and boil for a further 5 minutes.

Pack the garlic into small hot jars, pour the boiling liquid over the garlic, and seal the jars. Leave for about 6 weeks before using.

Spiced Gooseberries

Sweet and pleasantly spicy and ideal with cold meats, with chicken and with game.

2 kg gooseberries
1 cup water
1 medium onion, finely chopped
2½ cups malt vinegar
1 tablespoon cinnamon
1 tablespoon ground ginger
1 teaspoon ground cloves
1.25 kg brown sugar
1 teaspoon salt

Top and tail the gooseberries. Place them in a large saucepan, add the water, and slowly cook for 15 minutes.

Add the remaining ingredients, mix well, and cook slowly for about 45 minutes, stirring often, until soft and thick.

Spoon into hot, clean jars and seal.

Makes about 2.5 litres.

Pickled Grapes

Use perfect bunches of purple grapes. Excellent to garnish chicken or duck or cold meat platters.

grapes
brown sugar
cider vinegar

Leave the grapes on the stem and take off any fruit that is marked or damaged. Put the bunches into clean jars without bruising. Make a syrup of equal parts of brown sugar and cider vinegar and boil for 5 minutes.

Warm the jars, either in a warm oven or in hot water — to expand the glass — then slowly fill the jars with the hot syrup and seal by the overflow method.

Let stand for 1 month before using.

Spiced Grapes

Rinse the grapes and use as an attractive and delicious garnish for meat platters or salads.

ripe black or green grapes
dry mustard
½ cup sugar
2 cups water
1 stick cinnamon
5 whole cloves

Make sure the grapes are perfectly sound and divide them into small bunches. Pack into clean, dry jars, giving each layer a good sprinkling with mustard.

Make the sugar syrup by dissolving the sugar in the water, over low heat, with the cinnamon and cloves. Boil for several minutes, then allow to cool and strain.

Pour the syrup over the grapes, seal tightly and leave for 3 months before using.

Makes 1 litre.

Pickled Kiwifruit

An attractive and delicious garnish for all hot and cold meats.

2 cups white vinegar
2 cups brown or white sugar
2 teaspoons whole cloves
2 teaspoons whole allspice
5cm stick cinnamon
1.5 kg kiwifruit

Combine the vinegar, sugar, cloves, allspice and cinnamon in a saucepan. Bring to the boil, stirring, and simmer for 5 minutes.

Peel the kiwifruit and cut them in half lengthwise.

Strain the syrup into a clean saucepan and discard the spices. Add the prepared kiwifruit and simmer, very gently, for 10 minutes. Carefully pack the fruit into hot, clean jars, cover with the syrup and seal the jars.

Makes about 2 litres.

Pickled Kumquats

The unique sweet-sour and strong citrus flavour of the kumquats is delicious with ham and pork or used in a sauce for duck and other game. It is great on ice-cream too.

24 kumquats
1 teaspoon salt
2 cups sugar
2 tablespoons golden syrup
¾ cup malt vinegar
12 cardamom seeds
8 crushed peppercorns
½ teaspoon ground cinnamon
¼ teaspoon ground allspice
12 cloves

Halve the kumquats and remove the seeds. Place the kumquats and salt in a saucepan. Add hot water to cover and place the saucepan on moderate heat. Bring to the boil, then reduce heat and cook very slowly, uncovered, for about 30 minutes or until the kumquats are tender. Drain kumquats, reserving the water, and allow to cool.

In a large saucepan combine the sugar, golden syrup, vinegar, cardamom seeds, peppercorns, cinnamon, allspice and cloves. Bring to the boil, then simmer, uncovered, for about 10 minutes. Remove the saucepan from heat and allow to cool. Strain into a clean saucepan discarding the flavourings.

Add the kumquats and the reserved kumquat water. Bring to the boil, stirring often, and cook very slowly for about 10 minutes or until the kumquats are almost transparent.

Ladle the fruit into hot, clean jars, then cover with the syrup, and seal. Allow to stand for at least 3 weeks.

Makes about 3 cups.

Hot Lime Pickle

Hot, spicy, sharp and oily, and excellent with curries and with cold meats and cheeses too.

6 limes
2 tablespoons salt
2 teaspoons chilli powder
1 tablespoon garam masala
2 tablespoons sugar
6 cloves garlic, crushed
½ cup oil
3 large onions, finely chopped
2 cups malt vinegar

Roughly chop the limes, discard the seeds, and place the limes in a large bowl. Mix the salt, chilli powder, garam masala, sugar and garlic together. Sprinkle the mixture over the limes and toss well to coat them thoroughly. Cover the bowl and leave the limes to marinate overnight.

Next day, heat the oil in a saucepan, add the finely chopped onions and cook them until soft but not browned. Stir in the chopped limes and their juices, and scrape out all the spices from the bowl. Cook the mixture in the oil, stirring continuously, for 15 minutes. Pour in the vinegar and bring the pickle to the boil. Cover the saucepan and simmer for 1 hour. Stir frequently to prevent sticking.

Spoon the pickle into hot, clean jars and seal. Ready for use in 2 weeks.

Makes about 1 litre.

Loquat Pickles

These are sharp and excellent with lamb and hogget or other fatty meats. The loquats must be ripe and unblemished. Once you have prepared the loquats, cover them with the spiced vinegar, otherwise they discolour very quickly.

2½ cups white vinegar
1 tablespoon sugar
1 teaspoon salt
1 tablespoon peppercorns
ripe loquats

In a saucepan combine the vinegar, sugar, salt and peppercorns. Bring to the boil, then strain and allow to cool.
    Prepare the loquats by trimming and removing the stones. Pack them fairly firmly into 500ml jars. As soon as the jar is full, cover it with the cold spiced vinegar. Shake out the air bubbles and add more vinegar, then seal. Let stand for about 1 week before using.
    Makes about three 500ml jars.

Pickled Lemons

Use the lemon halves to stuff any bird that is being roasted; use, chopped, in curries or in crayfish or seafood salads, and use the juice to flavour salad dressings.

5 medium lemons, washed and halved crosswise
1 cup salt
additional lemon juice

In a 5-cup wide-neck jar combine the lemons and the salt. Squeeze the juice from enough additional lemons to cover the lemons by about 1cm. Store at room temperature, uncovered, covering the jar and shaking the mixture twice a week, for 28 days. Discard any skin should it develop.
    Cover the jar tightly and use the lemons as required.

Lemon Oil Pickles

Slices of lemon preserved in olive oil are just great with curries, chopped into salads or used as a garnish for fish dishes. Use the leftover oil for salad dressings too.

lemons, sliced fairly thinly
salt
paprika
green peppercorns
saffron threads
olive oil

Place the sliced lemons in a bowl and sprinkle them with salt. Let stand overnight, then drain well.

Layer them in clean Agee jars. On each layer sprinkle some paprika and scatter a few green peppercorns. When almost full, add a few threads of saffron, then fill the jar to about 1cm from the top with olive oil. Cover the jar with an Agee seal and a ring band, screwed on tightly.

Place a folded cloth on the bottom of a saucepan, place the jar or jars in the saucepan, cover with cold water and slowly bring to the boil. Boil steadily for 30 minutes. Remove the jars from the saucepan and allow to cool.

Leave for 12 hours before removing the ring band, and make sure the jar is sealed. Keep for about 1 month before using.

Pickled Mangoes

These mango chips or mango pickles are quite sharp and are an excellent accompaniment to curries. They also taste delicious with cold roast pork or ham.

12 just-under-ripe medium mangoes
2 tablespoons mustard seed
2 tablespoons ground ginger
4 cloves garlic, chopped
12 black peppercorns
1 tablespoon salt
½ cup sugar
5 cups vinegar

Peel and cut the mangoes into slices free from stone and pack into clean preserving jars.

Combine the remaining ingredients in a saucepan, bring to the boil and simmer for 20 minutes. Pour boiling hot over the mangoes and seal the jars. Keep for about 1 month before using.

Makes about 2 litres.

Marrow Pickle

An excellent pickle to serve with cold meats. As soon as the pickle is cold it is ready to use.

2 kg marrow
salt
1½ tablespoons ground ginger
1½ tablespoons dry mustard
1½ tablespoons turmeric
12 shallots, finely chopped
6 whole cloves
300g sugar
6 cups malt vinegar

Remove the seeds and cut the unpeeled marrow into squares. Sprinkle with salt and let stand overnight, then drain well.

Combine the remaining ingredients in a saucepan and boil for 10 minutes, add the marrow and boil slowly until the marrow is tender. It can be thickened with a little flour mixed with vinegar but this is not really necessary.

Spoon into hot, clean jars and seal.

Makes about 3 litres.

Pickled Mushrooms

Popular served as hors d'oeuvres on toothpicks with cocktails. Add a few to a green salad or add some to braised beef, soups or stews. Or serve as a special salad by themselves. Use very fresh, very white mushrooms.

500g button mushrooms
½ teaspoon mace
2cm piece fresh ginger, finely sliced
6 black peppercorns
½ small onion, finely sliced
1 teaspoon salt
¼ cup sugar
white vinegar

Wipe the caps of the mushrooms, if necessary, and place them in a saucepan. Add the remaining ingredients with enough vinegar to almost half cover the mushrooms.

Slowly bring them to the boil, by which time the mushrooms will have given off a lot of juices and shrunk slightly. Allow to simmer for 1 minute, then pack the mushrooms into hot, clean jars, pour the hot liquid over and seal.

Makes about 1 litre.

Mushroom Pickle

A sweetish pickle great with cold meats or as a special salad.

250g onions
1 cooking apple
1 stalk celery
500g tomatoes
1 kg mushrooms
2 teaspoons salt
freshly ground black pepper
2 cups malt vinegar
1 cup sugar
2 tablespoons whole allspice

Peel and chop the onions, peel, core and chop the apple. Chop the celery, peel and chop the tomatoes. Wipe the caps of the mushrooms and slice them.

In a large saucepan combine the onions, apple, celery, tomatoes, mushrooms, salt, pepper, vinegar and sugar. Tie the allspice in muslin and add to the saucepan. Bring to the boil and cook gently, uncovered, for about 1 hour, stirring occasionally.

Discard the spice bag, spoon the pickle into hot, clean jars and seal.

Makes about 2.5 litres.

Mustard Pickles

A good sharp, yellow mustard pickle.

3.5 kg mixed vegetables (cauliflower in small flowerets, sliced
green beans, peeled and cubed cucumber, chopped green
tomatoes)
500g onions, chopped
1½ cups salt
4 litres water
1 cup flour
6 tablespoons mustard

1 tablespoon turmeric
1 tablespoon curry powder
1 cup sugar
3 litres white vinegar

Combine the prepared vegetables in a large bowl. Sprinkle with the salt, pour over the water and let stand overnight.

Next day, drain the vegetables well, pour boiling water over them and drain again. In a bowl combine the remaining ingredients, except the vinegar, and mix to a smooth paste with some of the cold vinegar.

In a preserving pan put the remaining vinegar and bring it to the boil. Slowly stir in the mustard mixture and cook, stirring, for a few minutes. Add the vegetables, bring to the boil, stirring often, and simmer for 5 minutes, stirring occasionally. If the mixture is too thick add a little more vinegar.

Spoon into hot, clean jars and seal.
Makes about 8 litres.

Nasturtium Capers

Capers are actually the pickled flowerbuds of a wild Mediterranean shrub. They are expensive but a reasonable substitute, that almost tastes like capers, is pickled nasturtium seeds.

1 cup white vinegar
1 tablespoon salt
1 teaspoon sugar
½ bay leaf
4 black peppercorns
4 cloves
a little grated horseradish
green nasturtium seeds

Combine the vinegar, salt, sugar, bay leaf, peppercorns, cloves and horseradish in a saucepan. Bring to the boil, then allow to cool. Put the vinegar mixture in a clean 500ml jar.

Add the separated nasturtium seeds, as gathered, until the jar is full. Leave for about 6 weeks before using as capers.

Pickled Okra

The smaller the okra the better the pickle. Use with the hors d'oeuvres platter, as a meat garnish, or heat and serve with grilled or fried fish.

300g okra (approx., depending on the size)
1 each red and green chilli peppers
½ teaspoon dill seed
1 clove garlic, peeled
2 cups white vinegar
½ cup sugar
¼ cup salt

Soak the whole okra in iced water for 4–5 hours before making the pickle.

Pack the drained and dried okra into a hot, clean 1-litre jar. Place the chilli peppers, dill seed and garlic on top of the okra.

Bring the vinegar, sugar and salt to the boil and pour over the okra. Seal by the overflow method.

Makes 1 litre.

Pickled Olives

Pickling green olives is a very long and involved process to remove the bitterness. It is much easier to allow the olives to ripen until black and soft and then pickle them this way.

Pick over the ripe olives and discard any damaged or partly eaten — the birds love them — fruit. Wash the olives in several changes of cold water and drain well.

Bring to the boil enough brine to well cover them in the proportion of 5 teaspoons salt to 2 cups water. Drop the olives into the rapidly boiling brine, then quickly bring the brine back to the boil and boil the olives for 1 minute.

Remove the olives, allow to dry and let the brine cool. Pack the olives into clean jars, cover with the cold brine, put a layer of olive oil on top and cover the jars tightly.

Brown Pickled Onions

Leave these sweet and strong onions for one week and then you can indulge yourself. The longer they are left, the browner and the stronger they become.

5 kg pickling onions
250g salt
1 kg brown sugar
1 kg golden syrup
3 tablespoons black peppercorns
2 tablespoons whole cloves
6 dried small red chillies
7 cups malt vinegar

Peel the onions, place in a large bowl and sprinkle with the salt. Let stand overnight.

In a saucepan combine the sugar, golden syrup, peppercorns, cloves, chillies and vinegar, and bring to the boil. Allow to cool overnight.

The next day, drain and dry the onions thoroughly and pack them into clean jars. Pour the cold pickling liquid over the onions, dividing the spices among the jars, and cover tightly. Ready for use in about 1 week.

Makes about 10 litres.

Hot Pickled Onions

Hot, spicy yet very refreshing.

3.5 kg pickling onions
salt
5 cups water
5 cups white vinegar
150g sugar
2 whole cloves
pinch mustard seed
small stick cinnamon
1 bay leaf
1 clove garlic
sprig of thyme
3 tablespoons black peppercorns
3 red chilli peppers

Peel the onions, sprinkle with salt and allow to stand for 1 hour. Boil the water, then pour it over the onions, and allow it to cool. Drain the onions well, reserving the onion water, and pack them into clean jars.

Boil the remaining ingredients together with 5 cups of the onion water for a few minutes, then pour this mixture over the onions and seal the jars by the overflow method.

Ready for use in about 2 weeks, but better if kept longer.
Makes about 7 litres.

Sweet Pickled Onions

Sweet and succulent, you'll never be able to leave these alone until they're finished.

1.5 kg pickling onions
½ cup salt
1 or more red chilli peppers, seeded and quartered
½ teaspoon black peppercorns
4 slices fresh ginger

154

¼–1½ cups sugar (whether cocktail or sweet onions required)
7 cups white vinegar

Place unpeeled onions in boiling water to cover and let stand for 2 minutes. Drain, cover with cold water and peel.

Dissolve the salt in 4 cups cold water in a large bowl. Add the onions and enough additional water to cover, and let stand overnight. Drain, rinse in cold water and drain again.

Boil enough water to cover the onions. Add the onions and cook for 1 minute. Drain and arrange in hot, clean jars in layers with chilli pepper, peppercorns and fresh ginger.

Bring the sugar and vinegar to the boil, pour over the onions to within 1cm of top of jar and seal.

Makes about 2.5 litres.

Spiced Curried Onions

Coarsely chopped large onions save the laborious tear-jerking drama of peeling tiny pickling onions.

2.5 kg large onions
½ cup salt
500g brown sugar
1 tablespoon ground cloves
1 tablespoon ground allspice
2 tablespoons flour
1 teaspoon mustard
1 tablespoon curry powder
2 teaspoons turmeric
4½ cups malt vinegar

Coarsely chop the onions, place in a large bowl and sprinkle with the salt. Barely cover with cold water and let stand overnight. Drain the onions and pack them into hot, clean jars.

In a saucepan combine the remaining dry ingredients, then slowly stir in the vinegar. Bring the mixture to the boil and pour over the onions. Cover the jars tightly when cool. Ready for use in about 2 weeks.

Makes about 4 litres.

Spiced Orange Slices

An excellent accompaniment to hot or cold meats, especially ham and poultry.

5 large oranges
2½ cups white vinegar
500g sugar
2 teaspoons ground cloves
1 teaspoon ground cinnamon
whole cloves

Cut the oranges into thick slices and put in a large saucepan. Add cold water to barely cover the oranges. Bring to the boil and boil very gently for about 45 minutes, until the rind is tender. Remove the orange slices from the liquid.

To the liquid add the vinegar, sugar, ground cloves and ground cinnamon. Bring to the boil and cook gently for 10 minutes. Remove the orange slices with a slotted spoon and pack them into hot, clean jars, placing a whole clove in the centre of some of the slices.

Rapidly boil the syrup for about 30 minutes, until it thickens. Cover the oranges with the syrup and seal the jars.

Makes about 2.5 litres.

Pickled Green Passionfruit

Leave for a month before using as an unusual accompaniment to cold meats or fish. These are spicy with a slightly nutty flavour.

small green passionfruit
salt
spiced vinegar
sugar

Place the passionfruit in a bowl, sprinkle with salt and let stand overnight. Drain and dry the passionfruit. Pack them into clean jars.

Heat the spiced vinegar adding a tablespoon sugar to each cup vinegar. Place the jars of passionfruit in hot water to heat them, then pour the boiling vinegar into the jars to cover the passionfruit and seal.

Pickled Mountain Pawpaw

This is deliciously fascinating served on toothpicks with drinks. The pawpaw also makes an excellent meat garnish, and it is great with ice-cream too.

4 cups sliced, barely ripe mountain pawpaws
2 cups sugar
2 cups water
1 cup white vinegar
4 whole cloves
1 cinnamon stick
2 bay leaves
6 black peppercorns

Wash and slice the pawpaws discarding the seeds. Place in a saucepan, cover with water, bring to the boil and boil for 3 minutes. Drain.

Combine the sugar, 2 cups water, vinegar, cloves, cinnamon stick, bay leaves and peppercorns in a saucepan and bring to the boil, stirring occasionally. Add the pawpaw and cook very gently for 10–12 minutes, stirring very carefully. Remove the cinnamon stick.

Pack the pawpaw into hot, clean jars, cover with the syrup and seal.

Makes about 1.5 litres.

Pickled Peaches

An attractive and edible garnish for cold meat platters or hot meat dishes.

2 kg barely ripe peaches
2 cups white vinegar
1½ cups sugar
1 teaspoon ground cinnamon
½ teaspoon whole cloves

Peel the peaches and either cut them in half, discarding the stone, or slice them and discard the stone. This depends on the type of peach, whether or not it is a freestone variety.

In a large saucepan combine the vinegar, sugar, cinnamon and cloves. Bring to the boil and boil for 10 minutes. Add the prepared peaches and cook very gently until just tender. With a slotted spoon carefully remove the peach halves or slices to hot, clean jars.

Bring the syrup to the boil again and boil rapidly for a few minutes to reduce it slightly. Pour the hot syrup over the peaches, add a few cloves to each jar and seal.

Makes about 2 litres.

Spiced Peaches

The use of canned peaches ensures that these can be made at any time of the year. They are an unusual accompaniment to hot or cold ham, or to cold pork or chicken.

820g can peach halves, drained, with syrup reserved
1cm piece fresh ginger
½ teaspoon whole cloves
½ teaspoon whole allspice
1cm stick cinnamon
thinly peeled rind of ½ lemon
1 cup malt vinegar
½ cup brown sugar

Pour the peach syrup into a saucepan. Bruise the ginger with a rolling pin and crush the cloves and allspice with the back of a firm knife. Tie the ginger, cloves, allspice, cinnamon and lemon rind in muslin and add to the syrup. Stir in the vinegar and sugar. Bring to the boil, stirring to dissolve the sugar, then simmer gently for 10 minutes.

Add the drained peach halves and continue simmering very gently for 5 minutes. With a slotted spoon, remove the peach halves to warm, clean jars. Allow the syrup to cool, then remove and discard the spice bag. Pour the cold syrup over the peaches and seal the jars.

Makes about 2½ cups.

Pear Pickle

Great with cold meats or curries.

2 large onions
3 kg fairly hard pears
5 cups malt vinegar
2 cups brown sugar
½ teaspoon cayenne pepper
1½ tablespoons dry mustard
1½ tablespoons curry powder
4 tablespoons flour

Finely chop the onions, sprinkle with salt and let stand overnight. Drain well.

Peel, quarter and core the pears and in a large saucepan combine with the onions, vinegar, sugar and cayenne pepper. Boil very gently until the pears are just tender.

Mix the mustard, curry powder and flour to a smooth paste with a little vinegar and stir into the pickle. Cook for a few minutes longer.

When cold, spoon into clean jars and seal.

Makes about 3 litres.

Spiced Pears

Delicious with pork and ham and especially good when used with other spiced fruits to garnish the festive ham.

2 kg ripe pears
4 cups white vinegar
4½ cups brown sugar
long stick cinnamon
1 tablespoon whole cloves

Peel, quarter and core the pears.

Bring the vinegar, sugar, cinnamon and cloves to the boil and simmer for 10 minutes. Add the pears and poach them very gently until tender. This may only take a few minutes.

Carefully pack the pears into hot, clean jars, without crushing, then pour the strained syrup over the pears. Add a few cloves to each jar and seal.

Makes about 2 litres.

Pickled Peppers

Cut these delicious pickles into strips and serve as an hors d'oeuvre, add to salads or sandwiches, or use them for a salad by themselves. They also make an excellent garnish.

14 very ripe, sweet red peppers
1 cup white vinegar
2 cups water
1 cup sugar
2 teaspoons salt
1 teaspoon pickling spice (minus cloves and only 1 chilli)
cinnamon sticks

Wash, core and remove the seeds from the peppers and slice them into four lengthwise. In a saucepan combine the vinegar, water, sugar, salt and pickling spice. Bring to the boil and boil for 5 minutes.

Add the prepared red peppers to the syrup and simmer for

½ minute. Pack the peppers into hot, clean jars. Add a piece of cinnamon stick to each jar, cover to overflowing with the hot syrup and seal. Ready for use in about 3 weeks.

Italian Conserved Peppers

A superb way to preserve the colourful red and yellow peppers for use in the winter months. They make a marvellous first course or can be served on toothpicks with drinks.

red and yellow peppers
salt
dried basil
white wine vinegar
olive oil

Use large, fleshy and really ripe peppers and skin them by charring on all sides over a naked flame or under the grill, then washing off the skin under cold water. Make sure that all the skin is removed.

Cut the peppers in half and discard the stalk, core and seeds. Pack them into clean jars, sprinkling each layer lightly with salt and some dried basil. Cover the peppers with white wine vinegar and top with a thin layer of olive oil. Screw down the lid tightly.

To serve, drain the peppers well, then sprinkle with a little good olive oil and some freshly ground black pepper. Serve one pepper per person as a first course, with fresh brown bread.

Bread and Butter Peppers

These make an interesting change from the traditional **Bread and Butter Pickles**. Chill them and serve on fresh brown bread, or use as a salad or garnish, or in any way you would serve the cucumber variety. Use all three coloured peppers or any combination of two, or simply only one of the colours.

12 large green, red or yellow peppers
4 cloves garlic
1½ teaspoons salt
1 cup water
3 cups white vinegar
2 cups sugar
1 teaspoon mustard seed
1 teaspoon celery seed

Slice stalk end off the peppers, remove core and seeds and cut them lengthwise into thick strips. Place in a large saucepan, pour boiling water over them, bring to the boil and simmer for 1 minute. Drain.

Finely chop the garlic and with the side of the knife crush the garlic with the salt. Combine with the remaining ingredients in a saucepan. Bring to the boil and simmer for 30 minutes. Pack the drained peppers into hot, clean jars, then pour the hot liquid over and seal.

Makes about 3 litres.

Pepper and Pineapple Pickle

It sounds good and tastes good too. Tangy and sweet and quite mouth-watering served with grilled ham steaks, bacon or cold roast pork.

2 large green peppers
1 large cooking apple
350g onions
250g sugar
1 cinnamon stick
2 teaspoons dry mustard
2 tablespoons finely chopped fresh ginger
1 clove garlic, crushed
150g sultanas
400g can pineapple pieces
1 cup wine vinegar

Halve the peppers, remove the seeds and pith and coarsely chop the flesh. Peel, core and chop the apples and chop the onions. Mix the prepared ingredients in a large saucepan and add the sugar, cinnamon stick, mustard, ginger, garlic and sultanas.

Stir in the pineapple pieces and the juice, and the vinegar. Bring to the boil, cover the saucepan and simmer the pickle for 30 minutes, stirring often to prevent the pickle sticking. Remove the lid and continue to cook a further 15 minutes. Remove the cinnamon stick.

Pour the pickle into hot, clean jars and seal. Let stand for 1 month before using.

Makes about 1.5 litres.

Piccalilli

This popular pickle comprises mixed vegetables in a fairly thin mustard sauce. The pickle is light and mild and not as heavy as its American counterpart **Chow Chow**. The vegetables should be in recognisable pieces.

1 kg onions
1 small cauliflower
3 cucumbers
salt
malt vinegar
1½ teaspoons dry mustard
1½ teaspoons mustard seeds
1 teaspoon turmeric
1½ teaspoons cornflour
½ cup sugar

Peel the onions and cut into 2cm chunks. Cut the cauliflower into small flowerets, peel the cucumbers, remove the seeds if large, quarter them and cut into 2cm slices.

Place all the vegetables in a bowl, salt them thoroughly and let stand overnight. Strain the vegetables, rinse them thoroughly in cold water to remove the salt, then drain well. Place them in a large saucepan and almost cover with vinegar.

Mix the mustard, mustard seeds, turmeric and cornflour with a little vinegar and stir into the vegetables. Bring to the boil, stirring, and gently boil for 5 minutes. Stir in the sugar and cook for a further 7 minutes. Pour the Piccalilli into hot, clean jars and seal.

Makes about 4 litres.

Turnip Piccalilli

More like a mustard turnip pickle, this is superb with cheese or whatever takes your fancy.

1 kg swede turnips
salt
5 cups malt vinegar
6 whole cloves
6 small dried chillies
2cm piece fresh ginger, bruised
500g onions
50g sultanas
50g currants
3 tablespoons dry mustard
1½ tablespoons turmeric
2 tablespoons flour

Peel and chop the turnips into very small pieces, sprinkle lightly with salt and stand overnight. Next day, drain the turnips well.

Boil the vinegar, cloves, chillies and ginger for 15 minutes, then strain out the spices. Put the vinegar back in the saucepan and add the onions, cut the same size as the turnips, and boil again for 15 minutes.

Add the turnips, sultanas, currants, mustard and turmeric and boil very slowly until the turnips are tender. Mix the flour to a smooth paste with a little vinegar and stir into the pickle. Stir for a few minutes until slightly thickened.

Spoon into hot, clean jars and seal.
Makes about 2.5 litres.

Pickled Pineapple

Garnish and serve with ham, pork, sausages or fried fish. Or add some to chicken salad. Fresh pineapple could be used but it is much easier to use canned pineapple. If using fresh pineapple, substitute water for the pineapple syrup and cook the pineapple for 15 minutes longer.

3 x 450g cans pineapple slices
1 cup pineapple syrup
½ cup cider vinegar
1 cup sugar
2 teaspoons whole cloves
1 stick cinnamon

Drain the pineapple slices, reserving the syrup. In a saucepan combine 1 cup pineapple syrup with the vinegar, sugar, cloves and cinnamon. Bring to the boil and boil for 5 minutes. Add the drained pineapple slices and cook gently, uncovered, for about 30 minutes, until transparent.

Pack the pineapple into hot, clean jars, add a few of the cloves, pour the strained liquid over and seal.

Makes 1 litre.

Pickled Plums

Serve with cold meat, especially lamb or hogget.

3 kg red plums
2–3 cups malt vinegar
2–3 cups sugar
3 cinnamon sticks, broken
12 cloves
½ teaspoon ground mixed spice

Prick each plum here and there with a small skewer. Put in a bowl and cover with the vinegar. Drain off the vinegar and put in a saucepan with the sugar, allowing 1 cup of sugar for each cup of vinegar. Bring the sugar and vinegar to the boil, then add the cinnamon sticks, cloves and mixed spice. Boil for 20 minutes, then immediately pour over the plums.

Let stand for 3 days. Tip the plums and vinegar into a saucepan, leaving behind the sludge in the bottom of the bowl. Simmer the plums in the vinegar gently for 2–3 minutes. Bottle in clean jars when cold, and make sure the plums are completely covered in juice.

Spiced Prunes

Delicious with grilled sausages or steaks especially at barbecues, or by themselves as an appetiser.

500g stoned and cooked prunes
1 cup sugar
1 cup malt vinegar
½ teaspoon ground cinnamon
¾ teaspoon ground cloves

Place the drained prunes in a 1-litre screw-top jar.

Combine the sugar, vinegar, cinnamon and cloves in a saucepan, bring to the boil and simmer for a few minutes. Pour over the prunes and cover tightly when cool. Ready for use in 1 week.

Makes about 1 litre.

Pumpkin and Ginger Pickle

The smoothness of pumpkin and the tanginess of fresh ginger combine to make a pleasantly different and versatile pickle.

2.5 kg pumpkin
1 kg onions
salt
250g fresh ginger, finely chopped
2 litres white vinegar
2 cups sugar
3 tablespoons turmeric
2 tablespoons mustard seed
6 cloves
6 peppercorns
6 chillies

Peel the pumpkin and onions. Remove seeds from the pumpkin and cut the pumpkin flesh and onions into small pieces. Sprinkle with salt and let stand overnight. Drain well.

Combine the vegetables with all the other ingredients in a saucepan and simmer gently, uncovered, until the pumpkin is soft but not disintegrated.

Pour into hot, clean jars and seal.
Makes about 4 litres.

Quince Pickles

Extra good with cold or hot meats. The delightful pink colour makes a pretty pickle indeed. For best results use not-quite-ripe quinces.

quinces
white vinegar
white sugar
whole cloves
whole black peppercorns
cayenne pepper

Peel, quarter and core the quinces and cut into thick segments. Place the prepared quinces in a saucepan and two-thirds cover them with white vinegar. For every cup of vinegar used add 1 cup sugar, 4 cloves and 4 peppercorns, and add a pinch of cayenne pepper.

Bring to the boil and cook gently, uncovered, until the quinces are tender and a good pink colour. Allow to cool, then carefully spoon the quinces into clean jars. Cover with the syrup and seal the jars.

Sweet Spiced Rhubarb

Rhubarb is excellent when spiced and this ruby red relish goes extremely well with hot or cold roast lamb.

1 teaspoon ground cinnamon
½ teaspoon ground cloves
½ teaspoon ground allspice
½ teaspoon freshly grated nutmeg
1 cup malt vinegar
1 cup water
1 kg sugar
1.5 kg rhubarb
500g raisins

Tie the spices in a small piece of muslin and simmer with the vinegar, water and sugar for 20 minutes, stirring often. Remove the spice bag and add the rhubarb, cut into 2cm pieces, and the raisins and cook very slowly, stirring occasionally, until thickened. Some of the rhubarb should be more or less whole.

Put into hot, clean jars, allow to cool, and seal when cold.
Makes about 3 litres.

Pickled Shallots

Milder than pickled onions, these make an elegant substitute for their coarser brothers.

750g shallots
18 black peppercorns
3 bay leaves
3 teaspoons salt
3 tablespoons sugar
1 cup water
2½ cups white vinegar

Peel the shallots and place in a bowl. Sprinkle well with salt and let stand overnight.

Next day, rinse in cold water to remove the salt, then dry the shallots. Pack into 3 small preserving jars, and add 6 peppercorns and 1 bay leaf to each jar.

Bring the salt, sugar, water and vinegar to the boil and slowly pour over the shallots. Seal by the overflow method. Leave for at least 2 weeks before using.

Makes about 1.5 litres.

Pickled Snow Peas

Large flat snow peas are ideal for pickling and make great finger food with drinks. Or try adding a few to a green salad. The smaller, fat sugar peas are not really suitable.

1.75 kg snow peas
8 cups white vinegar
¼ cup salt
½ cup sugar
2 cups water
3 tablespoons whole pickling spice

Wash the pea pods, remove ends and string if necessary. Plunge them into boiling water and simmer for 5 minutes. Immediately rinse under cold water.

Combine the remaining ingredients in a saucepan and boil together for 10 minutes.

Pack the pea pods into hot, clean jars. Pour the strained vinegar mixture over them and seal by the overflow method. Ready for use in about 2 weeks.

Makes about 4 litres.

Pickled Tamarillos

Serve these whole or sliced in half with all lamb dishes, with roast meats or with curries.

1 kg white sugar
500g brown sugar
4 sticks cinnamon
3 cups cider vinegar
4 kg tamarillos

In a saucepan combine the sugars, cinnamon and vinegar, and boil them for 15 minutes.

Peel the tamarillos and add them to the saucepan and simmer for a further 5 minutes.

Pack into hot, clean jars, with a piece of cinnamon in each jar, and seal. Use after 1 month.

Makes about 5 litres.

Tomato Oil Pickle

Hot and spicy and excellent with curries. Ideal with cheeses too.

1½ tablespoons black mustard seeds
1½ cups malt vinegar
¾ cup chopped fresh ginger
20 cloves garlic, peeled and roughly chopped
20 fresh small green chillies
2 kg firm ripe tomatoes
1¼ cups vegetable oil
1½ tablespoons turmeric
4 tablespoons ground cumin
1 tablespoon chilli powder
1 cup sugar
1 tablespoon salt

Soak the mustard seeds in the vinegar overnight. Next day, grind to a purée in a blender. Add the ginger and garlic and purée with the mustard and vinegar.

Cut the chillies in half lengthwise and remove the seeds. Peel and chop the tomatoes.

Heat the oil in a large saucepan until smoking hot. Allow to cool slightly, then add the turmeric, cumin and chilli powder and fry, stirring, for a few minutes. Add the tomatoes, chillies, blended vinegar mixture and the sugar and salt.

Bring to the boil and cook gently, uncovered, until the tomatoes are reduced to a pulp and the oil starts to float on top. Taste and add more salt if necessary.

Allow to cool, then pour into clean jars and seal. Ready for use in 1 week.

Pickled Green Tomatoes

These whole pickled green tomatoes are hot and sharp and great with roast meats, especially lamb.

3 kg small green tomatoes
7 cups malt vinegar
2 cups sugar
1 tablespoon ground cloves
1 tablespoon ground allspice
1 teaspoon cayenne pepper

Choose even-sized tomatoes. Prick well with a fork, sprinkle with salt and let stand on a dish overnight. Next day, drain the tomatoes well.

Combine the tomatoes with the other ingredients in a large saucepan. Bring to the boil, then simmer very, very slowly for 1½–2 hours, until the tomatoes are very tender but still whole. Turn them in the liquid from time to time.

Allow to cool, then carefully pack into clean jars, cover with the liquid and seal the jars.

Makes about 4 litres.

Green Tomato Pickle

Call it a pickle, a chutney or a relish, this is particularly tangy and goes well with rich meats and cheese.

3 kg green tomatoes
3 large onions
salt
5 cups water
7 cups white vinegar
500g sugar
pinch cayenne pepper
2 tablespoons whole cloves
2 tablespoons whole allspice
1 tablespoon mustard seed
small piece root ginger, bruised

Slice the tomatoes and onions, sprinkle them well with salt and let stand overnight.

Next day, drain the tomatoes and onions and place in a large saucepan with the water and 2 cups of the vinegar. Boil for 30 minutes, then drain, discarding the water and vinegar.

To the tomatoes and onions add the remaining 5 cups vinegar, the sugar, the cayenne pepper, and the spices tied in muslin. Heat gently, stirring to dissolve the sugar, then boil gently for 30 minutes.

Discard the spice bag and pour the pickle into hot, clean jars and seal.

Makes about 3.5 litres.

Garden Pickles

Crisp strips of pickled vegetables are great with drinks or as a special salad. Vary the vegetables if you wish.

1 green pepper
1 red pepper
2 stalks celery
8–10 courgettes
2 onions
¼ cup salt
2 cups white vinegar
1½ cups sugar
2 teaspoons mustard seeds

Seed the peppers and cut the flesh into strips. Cut the celery, the unpeeled courgettes and the onions into strips. Combine the vegetables in a bowl, sprinkle with the salt and pour over enough cold water to cover the vegetables. Let stand overnight.

Next day, drain and rinse the vegetables well.

In a large saucepan combine the sugar, vinegar and mustard seeds. Bring to the boil, stirring until the sugar is dissolved. Add the vegetables, bring to the boil again, then immediately place the vegetables in hot, clean jars, cover with the liquid and seal.

Makes about 2 litres.

Sweet and Sour Pickles

These crisp pickled vegetables are absolutely scrumptious.

2 medium cucumbers, cut into cubes
2 red peppers, cut into cubes
1 green pepper, cut into cubes
2 small carrots, cut into strips
6 small onions, peeled and quartered
½ cauliflower, cut into flowerets
¼ cup salt
2 cups white vinegar
2 cups sugar
¼ teaspoon turmeric
2 teaspoons celery seeds
1 tablespoon mustard seeds

Sprinkle the vegetables with the salt and let stand overnight. Drain the vegetables and rinse them under cold water.

In a large saucepan combine the remaining ingredients and stir over low heat until the sugar dissolves. Bring to the boil, add the vegetables and bring back to the boil. Remove from heat immediately. It is best to put the vegetables into a basket or strainer before putting into liquid as it is very easy to overcook.

Pack the vegetables into hot, clean jars. Pour over enough of the vinegar liquid to cover, then seal the jars.

Makes about 2.5 litres.

Swedish Pickled Vegetables

Not only a pretty pickle but a delicious one too. Serve with drinks, with cold meats or as a salad.

1 small cabbage
3 medium carrots
4 green peppers
4 red peppers
500g onions
¼ cup salt
2¼ cups sugar
3 teaspoons mustard seeds
3 teaspoons celery seeds
pinch cayenne pepper
4 bay leaves
4 cups white vinegar

Shred the cabbage and finely slice the carrots, peppers and onions. Put all the vegetables in a large bowl. Sprinkle with the salt and mix well. Cover and let stand overnight. Drain well but do not rinse. Pack the vegetables into clean jars and stand in hot water to heat the jars.

Combine the remaining ingredients in a large saucepan. Stir over heat until the sugar is dissolved. Bring to the boil and simmer for 5 minutes. Pour the hot spiced vinegar slowly over the vegetables in the warmed jars, making sure the vegetables are covered. Seal when cold.

Makes about 4 litres.

Pickled Walnuts

Pickled walnuts are sheer bliss with a sharp cheese or with cold meat. Gather the green immature walnuts when they are about the size of large olives. They must be picked before the walnut shell begins to form inside the green casing. This could be from early November to mid-December depending on the weather and the part of the country where the walnuts are grown. A pin prick will soon tell you if it is too late.

100 green walnuts
salt
cold water
50g black peppercorns
75g fresh ginger, bruised
75g whole cloves
50g mustard seed
2.5 litres malt vinegar

Prick the walnuts all over with a pin. Prepare a brine with 175g salt and 2.5 litres cold water, and put the walnuts in it. Change the brine every 3 days for 9 days. Stir the walnuts frequently.

Remove the walnuts, drain them, then expose them to the sun for several days, until they turn black all over.

Boil together the peppercorns, ginger, cloves, mustard seed and vinegar for 10 minutes.

Pack the walnuts into clean jars, strain the hot vinegar over them and seal.

Walnut Pickle

Quite delicious with cold roast meats or cheese. The texture and flavour are especially complementary to soft cheeses such as brie or camembert.

1 medium onion
500g walnut pieces
4 tablespoons olive oil
2 teaspoons salt
½ teaspoon freshly grated nutmeg
½ teaspoon paprika
150g brown sugar
2 cloves garlic, crushed
25g fresh ginger, grated
1 large cooking apple, peeled, cored and sliced
1 cup malt vinegar

Finely chop the onion and any large walnut pieces. Heat the oil in a saucepan and cook the onion and nuts over a low heat, stirring occasionally, until the onion is soft but not browned. Add all the remaining ingredients and bring the pickle to the boil.

Cover the saucepan and cook gently for about 15–20 minutes, stirring often to prevent sticking to the saucepan. Spoon into hot, clean jars and seal. Leave for 2 weeks before using.

Makes about 1.5 litres.

Pickled Watermelon Balls

The watermelon retains its characteristic crispness to make a superbly edible garnish for meats or something different to serve on toothpicks with drinks.

10 cups watermelon balls
2 litres cold water
½ cup salt
3 small lemons, finely sliced
4½ cups sugar
2 tablespoons chopped crystallised ginger
2 cups white vinegar

Soak the fruit in the water and salt overnight. Drain and rinse well in cold water.

In a saucepan place the lemons, sugar, ginger and vinegar. Bring to the boil and add the fruit. Cook very slowly for about 20 minutes, until the syrup is clear.

Pack the fruit into hot, clean jars, then rapidly boil the syrup for about 10 minutes, until it thickens. Pour the syrup over the fruit and seal the jars.

Makes about 2 litres.

Watermelon Rind Pickle

This is an intriguing sweet pickle ideal with cold meats. It is almost like candied rind and can actually be finely chopped for use in fruit cakes or as a topping for ice-cream.

750g prepared watermelon rind
4 tablespoons salt
4 cups water
3 cups sugar
1½ cups cider vinegar
1 tablespoon whole allspice
2 teaspoons whole cloves
2 sticks cinnamon
2 teaspoons chopped preserved ginger

Prepare the watermelon rind by removing all the pink flesh and the hard outer green skin from the rind of a firm watermelon. Cut the remaining rind into 2cm cubes. Sprinkle with the salt, pour the water over and let stand overnight.

Next day, drain the watermelon and rinse well under cold water. Place the rind in a saucepan, barely cover with water and simmer for about 10 minutes or until the rind is tender. Drain.

Bring the sugar, vinegar, spices and ginger to the boil, stirring until the sugar is dissolved, and boil for 10 minutes. Strain and add to the rind. Bring to the boil again and continue to simmer until the rind becomes transparent. Pack into hot, clean jars and seal.

Makes about 1 litre.

The Refrigerator Pickles

This term, which originated in America, describes pickles that have only a short life and so are stored under refrigeration. The style of these fresh or marinated pickles probably originates in the Orient, where pickles and chutneys are usually made to be eaten immediately, rather than kept for later use. For this reason the refrigerator pickles use fewer spices and less vinegar and therefore are not as sharp as long-keeping pickles.

In most cases they taste better when brought up to room temperature rather than being served chilled. Their length of life has not been given in the recipes, as this could vary considerably depending on the age and condition of the fresh ingredients used, and different temperatures. Most refrigerator pickles are safe up to a week after being made, but some could keep for much, much longer. After a week, check the pickles and if in doubt do not hesitate to discard them.

Refrigerator pickles make great snacks, are superb finger food or toothpick food with drinks, and many can be served as special salads, too.

Not only are there refrigerator or fresh pickles but there are many refrigerator or fresh chutneys too. These are generally used as curry accompaniments but can also be used as normal chutneys. A simple example is a combination of sliced onion, sliced tomatoes and fresh coriander. There are, however, hundreds of fresh chutneys — almost enough for a book in themselves.

Pickled Blackeye Beans

Refrigerate for at least 2 days or up to 2 weeks before using these as a salad or side dish. Any dried beans could be used or even a combination of dried beans.

500g dried blackeye beans
1 medium onion, halved and thinly sliced
1 clove garlic, split
½ teaspoon salt
cracked or freshly ground black pepper
1 cup salad oil
¼ cup wine vinegar
chopped parsley to garnish

Wash the beans well and soak them in water overnight.

Next day, bring them to the boil in the same water and simmer very gently, until just cooked. Do not overcook otherwise they'll go mushy. Drain and cool.

Add the remaining ingredients and mix thoroughly. Refrigerate until ready to use. When serving, discard the garlic and garnish the beans with chopped parsley.

Makes about 6 cups.

Carrot Relish

A superb sweet-sour relish that keeps for weeks in the refrigerator. Serve as a salad or as an accompaniment to ham, pork or chicken.

1 kg carrots
1 green pepper
1 medium onion
2 cups tomato soup
1 cup sugar
¾ cup white vinegar
½ cup salad oil
1 teaspoon dry mustard
1 teaspoon worcestershire sauce

Scrape and thinly slice the carrots and cook them in a minimal amount of water for about 15–20 minutes, or until they are tender. Drain and allow to cool.

Finely chop the green pepper and the onion and add to the cold carrots.

In a saucepan combine the tomato soup, sugar, vinegar, oil, mustard and worcestershire sauce. Heat and bring to the boil, then pour the hot sauce over the vegetables. Mix well, allow to cool, then refrigerate until ready to serve.

Makes about 2 litres.

Dilled Carrot Sticks

Serve as a spicy salad or as nibbles with drinks.

1.5 kg carrots
2 tablespoons pickling spice
2 tablespoons dill seed
5 cups white vinegar
1½ cups sugar
1 clove garlic, chopped
6–8 sprigs fresh dill

Peel and cut the carrots into sticks. Cook in salted water for 2 minutes. Drain, place in a bowl and allow to cool.

Tie the spice and dill seed in muslin and combine in a saucepan with the vinegar and sugar. Bring to the boil, stirring constantly. Reduce heat and simmer for 5 minutes. Remove the spice bag and pour the hot syrup over the carrots. Allow to cool and refrigerate overnight.

Remove the carrots from the syrup and pack into hot, clean jars. Divide the garlic and dill evenly among the jars. Boil the syrup for 1 minute, then pour it over the carrots. Cover, allow to cool and refrigerate for several days before using.

Makes about 2 litres.

Cucumber Pickles

These paper-thin, mildly sweet pickles do not need bottling and stay very crunchy for about 3 weeks in the refrigerator. They make an excellent salad or addition to the hors d'oeuvres platter.

2 unpeeled telegraph or standard cucumbers, thinly sliced
1 medium green pepper, finely chopped
1 medium onion, finely chopped
1 tablespoon salt
2 teaspoons celery seeds
¾ cup sugar
½ cup white vinegar

In a bowl combine the cucumbers with the green pepper and onion. Sprinkle with the salt and let stand for 1 hour. Gently stir several times. Drain.

Combine the celery seeds, sugar and white vinegar and stir to dissolve the sugar. Pour over the vegetables and stir to blend. Cover and refrigerate.

Makes about 5 cups.

Frozen Cucumber Pickles

Not a refrigerator pickle, this one is a *freezer* pickle. It is simple yet absolutely scrumptious served with drinks or as a snack.

10 cups sliced unpeeled cucumbers
1 medium onion, sliced
2 tablespoons salt
1½ cups sugar
1 cup white vinegar

Combine the cucumbers, onion and salt. Refrigerate for 24 hours. Drain and add the sugar and vinegar. Refrigerate again for 24 hours, then put in small cartons and freeze. Serve not quite thawed out, so that the ice is still crunchy.

Pickled Horseradish

This is an excellent way to keep horseradish. The drained horseradish can be used in many recipes where fresh horseradish is needed or mix it with sour cream or whipped cream and serve with roast beef, steaks or fish.

horseradish roots
white vinegar
salt

Scrub the horseradish, peel it, then mince or grate it. Pack into clean jars and cover with a combination of 2 cups white vinegar and 1 teaspoon salt.
    Cover and store in the refrigerator.

Kim Chee

This is a Korean recipe, used as a pickle or as a garnish. The pickle is strong smelling so keep it tightly covered in the refrigerator.

1 fresh Chinese cabbage or celery cabbage
½ cup salt
2 spring onions, finely sliced
3 small cloves garlic, finely chopped
3 tablespoons seeded and chopped red chilli peppers
1 tablespoon sugar
1 teaspoon grated fresh ginger
4 cups water

Cut the cabbage into 4cm lengths. Mix in the salt, add water to cover, and let stand for 4 hours.

Drain the cabbage well — it should be limp — and combine with the remaining ingredients. Pack into clean containers and cover well. Refrigerate for at least 2 days before serving.

Makes about 6 cups.

Marinated Pickled Mushrooms

Tarragon gives these juicy morsels a lively flavour. They keep well refrigerated and can be served on toothpicks with small squares of buttered brown bread, along with other finger food, with drinks. Or they can be served as a salad.

500g very fresh small button mushrooms
juice of 1 lemon
¼ cup tarragon vinegar
¼ cup olive oil
1 tablespoon dried tarragon
2 cloves garlic, finely chopped
1 tablespoon coriander seed
4 bay leaves
10 whole allspice
10 black peppercorns
2 cups water

Wipe the mushrooms with a damp cloth. Sprinkle them with the lemon juice and toss well.

Combine the rest of the ingredients in a saucepan, bring to the boil and simmer for 5 minutes.

Working in batches, place some of the mushrooms in the liquid and gently poach for 1 or 2 minutes only. Quickly remove with a large slotted spoon and place in a bowl. Poach all the mushrooms and allow to cool.

Rapidly boil the liquid in the saucepan until it is reduced to about 1 cup. Cool the liquid and pour it over the mushrooms, making sure you include all the spices in the bottom of the saucepan. Refrigerate for at least 24 hours before using.

Chinese Radish Pickles

Excellent served with halved or quartered hard-boiled eggs.
Chunks of cucumber can also be prepared this way, separately
from the radishes, otherwise they'll stain a hideous pink.

2 bunches small red radishes
1 tablespoon salt
1 cup water
½ cup white vinegar
2 medium-sized fresh chillies, chopped
1 tablespoon white sugar
1 tablespoon finely chopped fresh ginger
dash brandy
some yellow mustard seed

Wash and trim the radishes and cut a cross into the root ends.
Combine the other ingredients and steep the radishes in the
mixture for about 5 hours. Serve with drinks.

Pickled Turnips

These Japanese-style pickles are best stored for a few days
before serving with drinks, or as a salad.

700g small white turnips or daikon
2 tablespoons salt
1 cup white vinegar
¾ cup sugar
½ teaspoon yellow food colouring
¼ teaspoon paprika

Peel the turnips and cut crosswise in thin slices not more than
0.5cm thick. Mix with the salt and let stand for 1 hour. Drain
and rinse thoroughly with water.

Bring remaining ingredients to the boil. Add turnips and
simmer for 2 minutes. Cool, then refrigerate until ready to use.
Serves 8.

Garlic Mixed Pickled Vegetables

Serve these delightful pickles as a salad or, better still, by themselves as a first course. The combination of green, white and purple-black looks stunning too.

1 cup olive oil
1½ cups white vinegar
4 cloves garlic, crushed
⅓ cup sugar
salt and pepper
8 cups mixed vegetables — whole green beans, topped and tailed, cauliflower, cut into flowerets, white turnip, peeled and sliced, green peppers, sliced thick, asparagus, hard stalk removed, mushrooms, halved or caps only, and black olives, the more shrivelled, the better

Boil the oil, vinegar, garlic, sugar and salt and pepper for 5 minutes. Place the vegetables in a basin, pour the boiling liquid over them and gently toss in the liquid. Allow to cool, turning the vegetables occasionally. When cold, transfer the vegetables and liquid to a large screw-top jar and refrigerate for at least 24 hours. Upend the jar occasionally.

When serving, restore vegetables to room temperature so that dressing will liquefy.

Serves 8–10.

Italian Pickled Vegetables

Serve these sharp pickles with drinks or as a salad or as a snack.

4 cups prepared vegetables — cauliflower flowerets, sliced carrots, chopped green or red peppers, quartered artichoke hearts, green beans cut in thirds, sliced bulb fennel, or white mushrooms halved or left whole
2 tablespoons olive oil
basil, thyme, rosemary and garlic
wine vinegar
water

190

Prepare a selection of vegetables and put in a 4 or 5-cup screw-top jar. Add the olive oil, and the herbs — fresh if possible — then fill the jar with equal amounts of wine vinegar and water. Put the top on the jar and refrigerate for a minimum of 2 days, upending the jar occasionally.

Marinated Pickled Vegetables

Serve as finger food at parties, or as part of a first course platter or as a special salad.

½ medium cauliflower
500g broccoli
12 medium mushrooms
1 red pepper
3 medium carrots
2 cloves garlic, crushed
¾ cup oil
½ cup wine vinegar
1 tablespoon sugar
1 teaspoon salt
1 teaspoon dry mustard
1 teaspoon dried basil
¾ teaspoon freshly ground black pepper
⅛ teaspoon freshly grated nutmeg

Cut the cauliflower and broccoli into flowerets. Cut the mushrooms in half and the pepper into strips. Peel and diagonally slice the carrots. Combine the vegetables in a large airtight container.

In a bowl combine the remaining ingredients and mix well. Pour the marinade over the vegetables. Stir or shake well to make sure all the vegetables are coated with the marinade. Cover and refrigerate at least overnight but preferably for several days, occasionally tossing the vegetables in the marinade.

Middle Eastern Pickled Turnips

A perfect flavour and texture to enjoy with pre-dinner drinks. The addition of the beetroot not only gives the turnips a fascinating pink colour but also adds to the taste.

1 kg small white turnips
a few celery leaves
4 cloves garlic, peeled
1 medium beetroot, peeled and sliced
4 tablespoons salt
3 cups water
1 cup white wine vinegar

Peel the turnips and cut them into halves or quarters, depending on the size. Pack the pieces of turnip into a large clean jar with some celery leaves and the cloves of garlic. Place slices of raw beetroot between the layers at regular intervals.

Dissolve the salt in the water and stir in the vinegar. Cover the vegetables with this solution and cover the jar tightly.

Store in a warm place — on the kitchen bench — until ready in about 10 days, then keep the pickles refrigerated. The pickles should be eaten within 1 month of making.

Makes about 2 litres.

Pickled Mixed Vegetables

Finger-pickin' good at the table or with drinks.

½ small cauliflower
2 large carrots
2 stalks celery
1 green pepper
100g pitted olives
¾ cup wine or cider vinegar
½ cup olive oil
1 tablespoon sugar
1 teaspoon salt
½ teaspoon cracked black pepper
½ teaspoon chilli paste
½ teaspoon oreganum
¼ cup water

Cut the cauliflower into flowerets. Peel the carrots, wash the celery, halve the green pepper and cut them into 5cm strips.

Combine all the ingredients in a saucepan. Bring to the boil and simmer, covered, for 5 minutes. Cool and refrigerate for at least 24 hours in a large screw-top jar. Gently shake or upend the jar occasionally.

Makes about 1 litre.

Chinese Pickled Vegetables

These simple pickles are superb at a party. Daikon is also known as Chinese radish or Japanese radish and is very similar to white turnip. The pickles should keep in the refrigerator for several weeks.

250g daikon or white turnip
3 carrots
4 small pickling cucumbers
1 green pepper
½ small cabbage
10 cups water
5 tablespoons salt
1½ tablespoons black peppercorns
6 slices fresh ginger
4 small red chilli peppers
¼ cup white wine vinegar

Peel the daikon and carrots, wash the cucumbers and cut into sticks about 4cm long. Halve the green pepper, remove seeds and core, and cut into bite-sized pieces. Cut the cabbage into small pieces. Allow the vegetables to dry out for 3–4 hours in the sun or in the hot water cupboard.

Bring the water to the boil, add the remaining ingredients, bring back to the boil, then remove from heat and allow to cool.

Place the dry vegetables in several large clean screw-top jars. Pour over the unstrained brine—the vegetables should be covered by the liquid—and refrigerate for several days before using. Upend the jars occasionally.

Makes about 3-4 litres.

Oriental Pickled Vegetables

Superb to pick at with pre-dinner drinks.

2 large carrots
2 small white turnips
3 stalks celery
6 whole cloves
6 black peppercorns
pinch ground cinnamon
2 fresh chillies or 4 dried chillies
1 teaspoon salt
1 teaspoon grated fresh ginger
½ cup white sugar
1½ cups cider vinegar

Peel the carrots and turnips. Thinly slice the carrots diagonally, halve the turnips and thinly slice them. Slice the celery on the diagonal.

In a saucepan combine the other ingredients, then bring them to the boil. Remove from heat and add the vegetables. Gently stir them for a few minutes, then allow to cool.

Put vegetables and marinade in a 1-litre screw-top jar. Cover and refrigerate for about 6 hours before serving. Upend or shake the jar occasionally to distribute the spices.

Makes about 1 litre.

The Jellies

There are three ways to make jelly: first, using the natural setting agent in fruit, the pectin; second, adding juice with a natural setting agent like lemon juice; and third, using gelatine or another commercial setting agent. The first makes the best jelly of course. The second makes a very soft jelly, almost pourable, and the third can be as soft or as firm as you prefer.

Pure fruit jellies, sometimes flavoured with wine or herbs, are great with hot or cold meats. Other jellies have differing uses but basically they all go with some sort of meat, poultry, game or fish. Guava jelly with roast lamb, redcurrant jelly with game, tarragon jelly with chicken, are a few of the classics.

The **Basic Fruit Jelly** is a way of making many fruits—apples, quinces, guavas and the like—into superb fruit jellies. The 'dos and don'ts' of making this type of jelly are listed there. The jelly bag or natural draining method is much preferred since it produces a beautifully clear jelly. It is often said that pushing the liquid through a sieve instead will save time, but the hour or so saved only produces a murky, cloudy, jam-like substance that is nowhere near as attractive as a crystal-clear jelly.

Although some jellies can be made from herbs, using lemon juice and sugar as setting agents, the surer method is to use a bland fruit which is high in pectin (like apples) as a base, and then flavour the jelly well with the desired herb.

A large, shallow saucepan allows rapid evaporation of the liquid, so that the setting point of the jelly is more quickly reached.

Remember that overripe fruit does not have so much pectin as slightly underripe fruit. The growing season will also affect the pectin and acid content of fruits. A wet growing season will lessen the pectin content, a dry growing season will increase it. Since the estimated yield is affected by the amount of pectin in the fruit, it is a good idea to have a couple of spare jars ready and sterilised when you make the jelly, in case the pectin content is unusually high.

Basic Fruit Jelly

Fruit jellies are great with all roast meats, with cold meats, with cheese or for use in glazing meats.

Use fruits rich in pectin such as apples, gooseberries, guavas, quinces, japonica apples, blackcurrants or redcurrants, loquats, crab apples, cranberries or plums, or combinations of these or with other fruits. Herbs and wine can be added as flavourings.

1.5 kg fruit
sugar

Coarsely chop the fruit if necessary and place it in a large saucepan. Fruit without lots of liquid such as apples, quinces, etc. should be barely covered with water. Berries and juicy fruits should only have a little water added. Bring the fruit to the boil and simmer until the fruit is very soft and all the juice has been extracted.

Place the pulp in a jelly bag or in muslin and allow the juice to drain overnight or for at least 2 hours. Do not squeeze the bag, otherwise the juice will be cloudy.

Next day, measure the juice into a large saucepan, bring it to the boil and skim if necessary. Allow 1 cup sugar to each cup of juice. Add the sugar and stir until dissolved, then boil rapidly until the setting point has been reached. Test after 5 minutes by placing a little on a cold saucer. If it jells it is ready. Keep testing every 5 minutes until the setting point is reached. When ready, pour into small jars and cover.

If it doesn't jell, simply reheat and boil until it is ready. If it is too solid, reheat and dilute with a little water, then allow to reset.

Spiced Gooseberry Jelly

An intriguingly dark jelly, ideal with cold meats.

1 kg gooseberries
2 cups malt vinegar
1.5 kg brown sugar
1 tablespoon ground allspice
1 tablespoon ground cloves
1 tablespoon ground cinnamon

Top and tail the gooseberries, wash and drain them.

Combine the gooseberries in a large saucepan with the remaining ingredients, bring to the boil and simmer, uncovered, very slowly for 2 hours. Stir often, especially towards the end of cooking.

Blend in batches in a blender to produce a thick purée. Pour into hot, clean jars and seal when cold.

Makes about 1.5 litres.

Gooseberry Mint Jelly

Perfect with cold meats, especially lamb or hogget.

ripe gooseberries
white sugar
fresh mint

Wash gooseberries and put in a saucepan. Nearly cover with cold water. Bring to the boil and simmer until pulpy. Strain through a sieve, pushing as much through as possible.

To each cup of gooseberry purée add ¾ cup sugar. Add a large bunch of mint tied in a bundle and boil for 10 minutes or until ready to jelly.

Remove mint, pour into small jars and cover.

Green Pepper Jelly

This colourful jelly is a favourite in the American south. It is a tangy and sweet accompaniment to meats and cheeses.

4 green peppers, seeded
1 red pepper, seeded
1 cup cider vinegar
750g sugar
½ teaspoon salt
juice of 2 lemons

Mince the peppers and drain them well.

Place the peppers and the remaining ingredients in a saucepan, bring to the boil and simmer for 10 minutes. Test for consistency as for fruit jelly. If not sufficiently set, continue to boil for a further 5–10 minutes, testing continually. Add a few drops of green food colouring if desired.

Place in small jars and cover.

Makes about 1 litre.

Mint Jelly

This is delicious with cold meats, especially mutton or lamb.

1 cup malt vinegar
1 cup water
2 tablespoons sugar
4 teaspoons powdered gelatine
1 cup finely chopped fresh mint

Bring the vinegar, water and sugar to the boil, stirring until the sugar is dissolved. Boil for a few minutes. Sprinkle the gelatine over a little cold water, let stand for a few minutes to soften, then stir it into the vinegar mixture until it is dissolved. Add the mint. Remove from heat and allow to cool, but not set.

Spoon into small, clean jars and cover.

Parsley Jelly

A sweetish jelly with a subtle parsley flavour. Especially good with smoked meats and smoked fish.

500g fresh parsley
cold water
juice of 2 lemons
sugar

Wash the parsley well and then press it down into a large saucepan. Barely cover with cold water, bring to the boil and simmer for 1 hour. Add the lemon juice and simmer a further 10 minutes.

Strain the liquid through muslin and return to the saucepan, discarding the parsley. Bring to the boil and for every cup of liquid add ½ cup sugar. Boil until it is ready to jelly, then pour into hot, clean jars and cover.

Tamarillo Mint Jelly

4 tamarillos
½ cup dry white wine
1 tablespoon gelatine
¾ cup white wine vinegar
2 tablespoons sugar
½ cup chopped mint

Cut the tamarillos in half and scoop out the pulp. Simmer the pulp in the wine until tender. Push as much as possible through a sieve.

Sprinkle the gelatine over the vinegar to soften. Add the sugar to the tamarillo purée and reheat. Stir in the gelatine/vinegar mixture and stir until well dissolved.

Allow the mixture to cool and when it reaches a syrupy consistency, stir in the mint. Refrigerate until ready to use. Cut it into cubes, put in a small serving dish and serve with lamb.

Serves 8.

Tarragon Jelly

Rosemary can be substituted for the tarragon.

2 kg cooking apples, or apple skins and cores
4 tablespoons fresh tarragon
1 cup white vinegar or half white vinegar and half dry white
*   wine*
sugar

Chop the apples — skins, cores and all — into a large saucepan. Add enough water to barely cover the apples, add half the tarragon and simmer for 45 minutes. Add the vinegar — or wine mixture — and boil for 5 minutes. Pour the apple into a jelly bag and let strain overnight or for at least 2 hours.

Measure the juice into a saucepan, bring to the boil and skim if necessary. For every cup of juice add 1 cup sugar. Stir until the sugar is dissolved, then boil rapidly until setting point is reached.

Sprinkle in the remaining tarragon and pour into small, hot, clean jars and cover.

Green Peppercorn Jelly

Make jelly as for **Tarragon Jelly** but omit the tarragon. Just before pouring the jelly into the jars to set, stir in 4 tablespoons rinsed green peppercorns. The peppercorns will float on the hot jelly so when it starts to set, stir the green peppercorns into the jelly.

Basil and White Wine Jelly

Make jelly as for **Tarragon Jelly** but use chopped fresh basil instead of the tarragon. Instead of the vinegar or wine/vinegar mixture use 1 cup dry white wine.

The Vinegars and the Sherries

The range of vinegars includes malt vinegars and white vinegars, cider, white wine and red wine vinegars, and sherry and champagne vinegars. These are the basic vinegars, their characters determined by their base ingredient.

Then there are the flavoured vinegars. These are basic vinegars flavoured with a herb, a fruit, a vegetable or a spice, to produce an aromatic vinegar which is used to give extra appeal to a great variety of foods and dishes. For instance, there is the classic tarragon vinegar so widely used in French sauces and dressings; or the raspberry, strawberry and other fruit vinegars that not only make vinaigrette dressing something special, or add interest to gravies and other sauces, but can also be used as a most refreshing drink when diluted with cold water. Mint vinegar can be used when fresh mint is unobtainable, and horseradish vinegar is useful in this way, too. Cucumber vinegar or shallot vinegar are both great when sprinkled on vegetables or on fish.

Most of the flavoured vinegars are perfect for de-glazing the frying or roasting pan, to make a sauce for the fry-up or roast. Or they can be mixed with dry mustard instead of the usual liquid to make a fascinating English mustard.

Try using flavoured vinegar to marinate and tenderise meat.

A touch of vinegar will disguise the fact that you have reduced the amount of salt in any recipe.

Like the flavoured vinegars, there are the flavoured sherries. These are obtained when a strong flavour has been soaked in a dry sherry to give it a particular taste. These sherries cannot be drunk, like some of the flavoured vinegars, but are used to add dash and interest to stews and casseroles, soups or Chinese dishes.

Experiment with these vinegars and sherries: they are great fun and quite a boon in the kitchen.

Blackcurrant Vinegar

Excellent in French dressing for salads, or for game and poultry sauces. A few teaspoons in a glass of ice cold water make a refreshing drink in the summer and in the winter a few teaspoons in hot water make a healthy drink.

1 kg blackcurrants
3 cups white vinegar
sugar

Bruise the fruit in a large bowl and pour the vinegar over. Let stand for 3 days, stirring occasionally.

Drain slowly, and to each 2 cups juice add 1 cup sugar. Bring to the boil and boil for 10 minutes.

Allow to cool before pouring into small, clear bottles.

Blueberry Vinegar

Excellent in chicken, chicken liver and meat marinades, or for deglazing the pan after frying or roasting chicken. Use instead of plain vinegar to make a different French dressing for salads.

Either fresh or thawed frozen blueberries can be used.

⅔ cup crushed blueberries
2 cups white wine vinegar

Place the blueberries and vinegar in a screw-top jar. Shake the jar each day for 3 days, then strain the vinegar and bottle. The vinegar is now ready for use.

Chilli Vinegar

Hot, hot, hot. Add a little chilli vinegar to whatever you feel
needs a lift — a salad dressing, a sauce, a soup, a casserole.

24 red chillies
2½ cups white vinegar

Cut the chillies in half and put them in a screw-top jar. Pour
over the vinegar and let the chillies infuse for 3 weeks, shaking
the jar often.

Strain the vinegar through muslin into small bottles and
seal. Float a dried chilli in each bottle to remind one of the
dangers of this vinegar.

Cucumber Vinegar

Great in dressings for green salads or fish salads and especially
good to flavour mayonnaise to go with seafood. Try it straight,
on fish and chips too.

finely sliced unpeeled cucumber
3 cups white vinegar
1 teaspoon whole white peppercorns
1 teaspoon salt
2 cloves garlic, chopped

Slice enough cucumber to two-thirds fill a 5-cup wide-necked
jar. Boil together the vinegar, white peppercorns and salt for
20 minutes, then allow to cool.

Add the garlic to the cucumber and pour over the cold
vinegar and peppercorns. Cover closely and let stand for 2
weeks, then strain into small bottles. Seal tightly and store in
a cool place.

Horseradish Vinegar

Ideal with freshly cooked mussels or other shellfish; or in dressing for coleslaw, rice salad or seafood; or sprinkled on any grilled or fried fish.

fresh horseradish
malt vinegar

Scrape the horseradish roots and mince them in a mincer or a food processor. Place the minced horseradish in an earthenware jar or jug.

Bring to the boil enough malt vinegar to cover well the horseradish, then pour it over. Loosely cover and let stand for 1 week. Strain the vinegar through muslin into bottles. Seal tightly and use when required.

The strained horseradish can either be discarded or used to make a mild horseradish sauce.

Mint Vinegar

Use for mint sauce when fresh mint is unobtainable or use in salad dressings, especially green bean salad and rice salad.

fresh mint leaves
malt vinegar

Place fresh, cleaned mint leaves in a large screw-top jar. Pack the mint loosely. Fill with malt vinegar, cover tightly, and let stand for 3 weeks.

Strain the vinegar, squeezing as much liquid out of the mint leaves as possible. Pour into clean bottles and cover tightly. Add a large sprig of blanched mint to each bottle for decoration before capping or corking.

Raspberry Vinegar

Excellent in vinaigrette dressing for salads, or in game sauces. It can also be sprinkled on fruit salad. Stir a teaspoonful into a glass of iced water to make a refreshing drink on a hot day.

Blackberries, boysenberries and peeled, chopped tamarillos can also be used this way.

500g raspberries
2 cups white vinegar
2 cups sugar

Place the raspberries in a bowl and add the vinegar. Cover and let stand for 1 week, stirring occasionally.

Strain the liquid without pressure into a saucepan and add the sugar. Bring to the boil and simmer for 10 minutes.

Allow to cool, then pour into clean bottles and seal.
Makes about 1 litre.

Rhubarb Vinegar

Excellent in salads or for deglazing the pan in which meat has been fried or roasted. Make sure the rhubarb is young and a good red colour, otherwise the vinegar will be too acidic and will not be a delightful ruby colour.

250g young, red rhubarb
4 cups cider vinegar or white wine vinegar
4 tablespoons sugar

Wash and trim the rhubarb and cut it into small pieces. Combine with the vinegar in a saucepan and sprinkle in the sugar. Bring to the boil, stirring occasionally, and cook slowly, uncovered, for 5 minutes. Allow to cool.

Strain through a double thickness of muslin into clean bottles, and seal.
Makes about 1 litre.

Shallot Vinegar

Extremely good in salad dressings or on fish and chips.

100g shallots
1 litre white vinegar

Peel and slice the shallots. Place them in a 5-cup screw-top jar, pour the vinegar over and let stand for 2 weeks, shaking the jar occasionally.
    Strain and bottle the vinegar.

Spiced Vinegar

A popular vinegar for use in salad dressings, this can also be used as a pickling vinegar when required.

5 cups white vinegar
1 tablespoon whole black peppercorns
6 thin slices fresh ginger
½ teaspoon whole allspice
2 tablespoons sugar
1 large onion, finely chopped
1 clove garlic, crushed
3 bay leaves

In a saucepan combine all the ingredients. Bring to the boil, then allow to cool.
    Strain into bottles and seal.

Strawberry Vinegar

A different vinegar to use in the dressing to make a green salad or a mushroom salad something special. Use it in chicken and game sauces or sprinkled on fruit salads. Or use, diluted with water, as a refreshing drink.

1 chip/punnet/container (500g) ripe strawberries
2 cups white vinegar
2 cups sugar

Wash and hull the strawberries and place them in a bowl. Mash them well, then cover with the vinegar. Let stand for 3 days, stirring occasionally.

Strain, rubbing as much through the strainer as possible, and put the liquid in a saucepan. Add the sugar, bring to the boil, stirring to dissolve the sugar, and simmer for about 10 minutes. Allow to cool, then pour into clean bottles and cover.
Makes about 1 litre.

Tarragon Vinegar

The classic herb vinegar with a wide variety of uses. This recipe can be used as a basis for other herb vinegars.

2 cups fresh tarragon leaves
4 cups white vinegar

Lightly bruise the tarragon leaves and place them in a large screw-top jar. Cover them with the vinegar and cover the jar. Let stand in a cool place for 7 weeks, shaking the jar occasionally.

Strain the vinegar into small bottles and place a sprig of fresh tarragon in each bottle. Cover each bottle tightly.

Thyme Vinegar

Here is an instant way of making herb vinegar. It can be used immediately but does improve with age. Like **Tarragon Vinegar** it can be used as a basis for other herb vinegars.

5 large sprigs fresh thyme
3 cups white vinegar
1 teaspoon sugar

Wash the thyme and shake off the excess water. Place the thyme, vinegar and sugar in a saucepan and bring to the boil. Simmer gently for 5 minutes.

Place the thyme in a warmed, clean 750ml bottle, gently pour in the vinegar, and seal.

Basil Sherry

Use as a delicious flavouring for soups, stews and casseroles.

fresh basil leaves
dry sherry

Break the fresh basil leaves into smallish pieces and fill a wide-necked bottle — a chemist's storage jar, or the kind you keep herbs and spices in. Cover with dry sherry, cork and leave for 10 days.

Strain off the sherry, pour it over fresh basil and leave it for a further 12 days. Strain again.

The sherry can now be added to savoury dishes, a spoonful or so at a time. Experiment with it!

Chilli Sherry

Use a few drops to give zest to soups, stews, casseroles and to Chinese foods too.

small fresh red chillies
dry sherry

Half fill a small screw-top jar with the whole fresh chillies. Fill the jar with dry sherry, cover and let stand for 3 weeks, shaking the jar occasionally.

No need to strain out the chillies, just use the sherry as required.

Ginger Sherry

Two condiments for the price of one. The sherry can be used to give Chinese dishes, salads or other dishes a fresh ginger flavour, and the ginger itself can be used for the same purpose.

fresh ginger
dry sherry

Fill a wide-necked, small jar with unpeeled, sliced fresh root ginger. Cover the ginger with dry sherry and cover the jar. Let stand for at least 1 week. The sherry will become strongly flavoured with the ginger. If the sherry gets too strong, top up the jar with more dry sherry.

The Mustards

There are two basic forms of mustard: whole mustard seeds and powdered or dry mustard. There are two primary types of mustard seeds that are available commercially — yellow (or white) and brown (or black) mustard seeds. Both are native to southern Europe. The yellow seed is considered milder than the brown seed. English mustard is a mixture of both seeds, American mustard uses the yellow seed and is coloured with turmeric, and Dijon-style mustard uses mainly the brown mustard seed. Grain or chunky mustards use either, or both seeds together. Powdered mustard and a Chinese mustard, *gai lat*, both use a combination of the two types of seeds.

There is also a true black variety of mustard seed which is milder in flavour than either the yellow or brown seeds. It is used mainly in curries, although in Sri Lanka, the black seed is made into a coarse ground mustard known as *abba*.

Although mustard seeds date back to biblical times and were much appreciated by the Romans, powdered or dry mustard is comparatively new. Powdered mustard as we know it today is said to be the innovation of an obscure old lady simply known as Mrs Clements of Durham. In 1729 she hit on the idea of grinding mustard seeds in the mill exactly like wheat and selling them in the form of a fine powder. This was most successful locally, and it is said she made a small fortune selling what became known as Durham mustard all over England.

The seeds — and the powder — in themselves are not 'hot' until liquid is added. Enzymes are then activated that produce the pungency. Dry mustard mixed to a paste with water loses flavour quickly and will not keep. If stored, it should be mixed with an acid liquid such as vinegar, beer or wine, which will stop the enzyme activity so that it retains its 'hot' quality. It does, however, develop a brown skin and loses pungency on standing. Herbs, spices or garlic may be added to enhance the flavour and oil may be added to improve the consistency.

Always mix mustard with the liquid at least half an hour

before using, so that it has time to develop its 'hot' flavour and also lose its raw taste.

Not only are both dry mustard and mustard seeds used in pickling as a flavouring but they act as a mild preservative, too. Dry mustard used in mayonnaise and salad dressings, to some extent retards the growth of bacteria. It also has an emulsifying effect.

Most of these mustards should keep a long time though some, where stated, should be kept under refrigeration.

As the saying goes, Mr Colman made all his money from the people who left mustard on the side of the plate. These mustards are a little too good for that, so use sparingly and eliminate the wastage.

Bought mustards can cost mega-dollars and usually taste nothing like a fresh home-made mustard. So try making your own at a fraction of the cost.

It is worth knowing that as well as being a delicious condiment, mustard is also a digestive stimulant.

Brown Seeded Mustard

Although brown mustard is strongly flavoured, this version is quite mild and pleasantly pungent.

200g brown mustard seeds
1 tablespoon salt
2 cloves garlic, chopped
freshly ground black pepper
white wine vinegar

Combine the whole mustard seeds, salt, garlic and pepper in a bowl. Add enough vinegar to cover well, mix and let stand for 2 days, adding vinegar as it is absorbed, until the mixture will absorb no more vinegar.

Purée the mixture in a blender, as if making a very thick mayonnaise, adding more vinegar if necessary.

Store in small, tightly covered jars. Ready for use immediately.

Chilli Mustard

For those who like their mustard *hot* but not deadly.

1 cup yellow mustard seeds
1 cup brown mustard seeds
2 tablespoons black peppercorns
1 tablespoon small dried red chillies
1 tablespoon salt
1½ cups white wine vinegar
1½ cups dry white wine
1 cup olive oil

In the blender process the mustard seeds in about four lots until they are well chopped, but not completely reduced to powder. As they are chopped, place them in a large bowl.

Blend the peppercorns and chillies until finely chopped and similar to coarsely ground black pepper. Add to the mustard. Add the salt, wine vinegar, white wine and oil, and mix well. Let stand for 24 hours to thicken. Spoon into small jars and cover tightly.

If you're really unafraid of hot things, then add another tablespoon of chillies.

Chunky Mustard

This mustard goes well with beef, ham or cheese, and mellows well with age. Instead of red wine, white wine or vermouth can be used. Curry powder can also be added, or the herbs varied.

125g yellow mustard seed
125g brown mustard seed
4 tablespoons whole black peppercorns
¼ cup olive oil
1 cup red wine
1 cup wine vinegar
4 teaspoons salt

1 teaspoon dried basil
½ teaspoon dried oreganum

In a blender combine both mustard seeds and blend for ½ minute or until the seeds are well chopped. Pour into a bowl. Blend the peppercorns until they resemble cracked pepper, and add to the mustard. Add the remaining ingredients. Stir well — it should be quite sloppy. Let stand overnight to thicken. If it is too thick add more olive oil.

Pack into small jars or crocks with lids. Store in a cool cupboard.

Grain Mustard with Fenugreek

Surprisingly, many people who are not keen on mustard enjoy this one. Fenugreek is an ingredient in most curry powders and gives the mustard a deliciously intriguing pungency. The finer you purée this mustard the hotter it will be. Do it in batches, varying the degree of blending from almost whole seeds to a mayonnaise-like consistency.

125g yellow mustard seeds
125g brown mustard seeds
75g fenugreek seeds
1 green pepper, finely chopped
3 cloves garlic, finely chopped
white vinegar

Combine the seeds, green pepper and garlic in a bowl. Add vinegar to well cover. When absorbed add more vinegar until the mixture won't absorb any more. This can take about 36–48 hours. Process the mustard in a blender until the desired consistency. Bottle in small, clean jars and cover tightly.

Green Peppercorn Mustard

Fiery and potent, this mustard is a must for mustard lovers.

½ cup yellow mustard seeds
2 tablespoons green peppercorns, rinsed
2 cloves garlic, crushed
½ cup oil
1 cup white wine vinegar
1 teaspoon salt

Combine all the ingredients in a bowl and let stand in a cool place — not the refrigerator — for 2 days.

In a blender coarsely purée the mustard in batches. Mix the blended mustard well and spoon into small, clean jars and cover tightly. Ready for use immediately.

Herb Mustard

This hot-sweet flavour is ideal with all foods that traditionally go well with mustard.

200g yellow mustard seeds
100g brown mustard seeds
20 whole cloves
1 tablespoon chopped fresh tarragon or 1 teaspoon dried tarragon
1 tablespoon chopped fresh thyme or 1 teaspoon dried thyme
¾ cup parsley sprigs
5cm piece root ginger, sliced
3 cloves garlic, chopped
⅓ cup honey
2 teaspoons salt
1 cup white vinegar
1 cup olive oil

In a blender combine the mustard seeds and blend until they are well chopped. Place in a bowl. In the blender combine the cloves, herbs, ginger, garlic, honey and salt, and blend until finely chopped. While blending, slowly add the vinegar and oil. Mix with the mustard seed, and stir until well combined. Cover and stand overnight.

If necessary, add more vinegar and oil; however, the mustard should be moist but not sloppy. Put into small jars and cover.
Makes about 3 cups.

Lemon Mustard

Hot and slightly lemony.

¾ cup yellow mustard seeds
1 tablespoon black peppercorns
½ cup lemon juice
½ cup dry white wine
½ cup oil
1 teaspoon salt
1 teaspoon sugar
1 teaspoon turmeric

Combine all the ingredients in a bowl and mix thoroughly. Let stand overnight.

Next day, transfer to a blender or food processor and blend or process until almost a purée.

Spoon into small jars and cover.

Spiced Grain Mustard

Hot and spicy for the more discerning mustard fan.

100g yellow mustard seeds
100g brown mustard seeds
1 teaspoon black peppercorns
1 teaspoon white peppercorns
2 teaspoons whole cloves
2 teaspoons whole allspice
4 teaspoons coriander seeds
½ teaspoon cayenne pepper
1 tablespoon paprika
1 tablespoon turmeric
1 teaspoon ground ginger
1 tablespoon salt
½ cup olive oil
2½ cups white wine vinegar

In a blender or coffee grinder, grind the seeds and whole spices, medium to fine. Combine with the remaining ingredients, mix well and let stand for 8 hours. If too thick, add some more vinegar. The mustard should be wet, with a little excess liquid, but not runny. Pour into small jars and cover tightly.

Tarragon Mustard

Pale green and powerful with the superbly elegant flavour of fresh tarragon. Excellent as an accompaniment to ham, pork, veal, chicken or beef.

1 cup fresh tarragon leaves, stems removed
1 cup yellow mustard seeds
1 tablespoon green peppercorns
1 tablespoon salt
1 cup tarragon vinegar
1 cup dry vermouth
1 cup sunflower or safflower oil

Place the tarragon leaves, mustard seeds, green peppercorns, salt and vinegar in a blender and blend for 1 minute. Slowly and steadily pour in the vermouth and oil and blend for 1 minute. Depending on the size of your blender, this may have to be done in two batches.

Pour into clean jars and cover.

Yellow Seed Mustard with Vermouth

A smooth and creamy mayonnaise-style mustard.

½ cup yellow mustard seeds
2 teaspoons green peppercorns
½ cup olive oil
½ cup white wine vinegar
½ cup dry vermouth

Combine all the ingredients in a blender and blend until the mustard amalgamates and thickens. Let stand for 24 hours. Mix the mustard well, spoon into small jars and cover.

Apricot Mustard

Delicious with the special occasion ham. It will keep for at least a month stored in the refrigerator.

1 cup dried apricots
2¼ cups water
3 tablespoons honey
2 tablespoons dry mustard
2 tablespoons dry sherry
1½ teaspoons curry powder
¾ teaspoon ground ginger

Soak the apricots in the water overnight.

Next day, bring them to the boil and simmer until they are very soft. In a blender purée the undrained apricots, then add the remaining ingredients and thoroughly mix. Pour into small, clean jars and cover. Refrigerate until ready to use.

Smooth Green Peppercorn Mustard

This is an emulsified mustard, strongly flavoured with green peppercorns, that should be kept in the refrigerator. It is great with smoked fish or as a dipping sauce for fresh vegetables as well as all the foods mustard goes so well with. Try it on buttered toast too.

3 tablespoons green peppercorns, rinsed
1 clove garlic, crushed
1 tablespoon powdered mustard
1 egg
1 cup oil
salt

Combine the well-drained green peppercorns, garlic, mustard and egg in a blender. Blend until a smooth purée.

Gradually add the oil until the mixture emulsifies and is thick. Add salt to taste and spoon the mustard into small pots. Keep in the refrigerator.
Makes about 1½ cups.

Lusty Mustard

Like most of the better things in life this mustard is hot and sweet. It will make almost anything taste good.

1 cup (100g) powdered mustard
1 cup white vinegar
2 eggs, well-beaten
1 cup sugar
pinch salt

Mix the mustard and vinegar together and let stand overnight.
Next day, stir in the eggs, sugar and salt and bring the mixture to the boil. Simmer very slowly, stirring constantly with a whisk, until the mixture coats a spoon. Allow to cool.
Pour into small jars, cover and keep refrigerated.

Sweet Cardamom Mustard

Delicious with meat terrines, meat loaves or in sandwiches with cheese or vegetables.

2 eggs
½ cup brown sugar, firmly packed
½ cup cider vinegar
¼ cup water
2 tablespoons powdered mustard
1 clove garlic, crushed
2 teaspoons flour
1 teaspoon ground cardamom
pinch ground cloves

Beat the eggs and combine all the ingredients in a saucepan. Stir constantly over low heat until the mustard is thick and bubbling. Allow to cool, then spoon into clean jars and cover tightly. Keep refrigerated until required.
Makes 1½ cups.

Index

224

225

226